Take

Control Of

Your Life

The CBT-Based Guide To Combat Anxiety, Depression and Overthinking, Learning To Resist Temptation and Find Your Comfort Zone. Program Your Mind with Mindfulness Meditation

By Drake Moore

Sommario

Introduction

Depression is a mood disorder. That means it is more than a typical mood-swing experience. The medical field considers depression a severe medical illness that negatively affects your feelings, your thoughts, your actions, and reactions.

Experiencing such feelings can hinder your ability to think straight and affect your daily work, which results in lost time, lost opportunities, and low productivity.

The disorder can also lead to emotional problems and difficulties with emotional management. Sometimes you may feel like life is not worth living, which is why many suicide victims have a history of depression that went unhandled effectively for too long.

It is vital to understand that depression is not a mental or emotional "difficulty" that one can "snap out of" at will or "get it together." Depression is not something you can take a nap for and sixty minutes later wake up depression-free. It surpasses the blues and mood swings and is a serious condition that gets worse the longer it remains unaddressed and untreated.

Since we are learning how to overcome it using a "treat ourselves" approach, you need to understand—and accept—that dealing with and overcoming the issue will call for time, and therefore patience, commitment, and all the effort you can muster. Simultaneously, you have to acknowledge that you cannot take a shortcut to emotional well-being. You have to work through the issue and overcome it, because if you do not, it is going to wreck your life!

To differentiate feeling blue and moody from depression, consider the following signs.

General Signs of Depression (Depressive Disorder)

The signs and symptoms of depression are often similar to those of mood swings and the so-called blues. However, the duration of the symptoms, or rather for how long they manifest, is the determinative factor that delineates the blues from depression.

Signs and symptoms of depression

At least two weeks of experiencing the following symptoms should be cause for alarm:

- Sleep disturbances and abnormal sleep patterns, insomnia, or oversleeping.

- Eating disorders, including reduced appetite leading to weight loss, or a sudden increase in appetite and cravings, especially for unhealthy foods, leading to weight gain.

- A constant sense of sadness, emptiness, or tearfulness.

- A bleak outlook of life: Feeling like everything is wrong and as if it will never get better. You start thinking about how nothing you do would make things better.

- Self-loathing: You always feel guilty and worthless. You continually beat yourself up for perceived faults and mistakes.

- Anger/irritability: You experience angry outbursts and get agitated often and usually over trivial matters. Most things and people get on your last nerves. You could shout at an innocent cat for climbing on the table, or yell at a toddler for doing something as normal as leaving toys on the floor.

- Feeling restless or slowed down.

- Difficulty focusing, making simple decisions, or recalling glaring details.

- Engaging in purposeless physical activity such as pacing, hand-wringing, knuckle cracking, fidgeting, etc. Usually, you are unlikely to notice when you engage in these behaviors, but other people will see it and may even mention it.

Chapter 1 Diagnosing Depression

The clinical definition of depression is easier explained by identifying the effects it causes on someone's life. The feelings may be different but they all fall under a category of sadness. Living with depression can ultimately impact your ability to function in society. It impedes on your capability to rest, socialize, work, and otherwise lead a normal life.

There are an abundance of causes behind the feelings of depression. If you are or have experienced a major life change you could possibly feel differently, saddened most often. This could be the demise of someone you know or love, loss of a job or a medical diagnosis that changes your life forever. These are just a few of the instances that could cause an onset of your depression.

Don't spend another minute or day waiting to feel better. It doesn't just happen. You must be proactive in seeking help and change. Your happiness and well-being depends on you and the guidance you seek. Your next move to overcome your issues will be a positive one and it will lead to a happier and healthier you.

People who live with depression often find it difficult to do things they once did with ease. It may be something that you found joy in doing and all of a sudden, it is almost impossible for you to do it now. You may feel a sense of loneliness, sadness, defeat and many other inexpressible feelings. This is just a sample of the emotions that those living with depression may encounter. Depression is a condition of the mind, heart and soul because it can affect them all. Your depression may look and feel entirely different from the depression of someone else. It has no face. There are no red flags that protrude from the head. Instead, it is identified by observing the acts and feelings of someone dealing with depression or anxiety, even if you must observed yourself.

Recognizing the Signs or Impacts of Depression

You may be or know someone battling depression but don't know the signs. It is hard to suggest that someone gets help if you aren't sure of the trials they are facing. In order to recognize depression, it helps to know the signs it presents or the changes it causes in one's life.

Once the signs are recognized, you should suggest or encourage help or counseling. Among the most familiar indicators of depression.

Crying unexplainably or without reason

Increased or extended periods of sadness

Excessive anger, aggravation or anxiety

Cynicism

Lack of motivation or depleted energy

Exhaustion without reason

Battling guilt or lack of self-worth

Find it difficult to remain focused or make decisions

No longer interested in things once enjoyed

Consistent pains or unexplainable aches

Repetitive thoughts of ending your life

If you experience or know someone who displays signs or symptoms as those stated above, it is likely that they are coping with depression. Once the signs have been recognized, it is time to intervene or seek help. You likely don't know what you should do or where to turn to for help. There are several resources available for people battling this issue.

Consider the following:

Contact your local mental health office

Conduct an online search for counselors or private practice mental health care providers

Speak with others you know who have overcome or are coping with depression

The following table will help you to distinguish between depression and just a bad day. While most people living with depression may appear to just be having an off day, continuous or consistent bad days are an underlying problem that must be faced.

A Bad Day	Depression
Had a bad night and can't get out of bed	Every day is bad and you lay around all day
Lost your job and it is hard finding strength to find another one	Lost your job over a year ago and can't seem to do anything but sleep and cry
Don't have anything to wear to an event so you decide to just stay home	Not interested in attending an event ever

	and always decline or ignore the invitation
Loss of appetite because you've got so many things that require your attention	Difficulty eating at all because you're facing too many challenges in life
Can't sleep because you depended on caffeine to get you through the hectic day	Most nights are sleepless and you have no idea why but days are spent sleeping in
Feeling guilty because you missed your best friend's birthday	Feeling guilty but not sure why and can't seem to overcome the feeling
Crying because you lost your pet or suffered another sentimental loss	Crying when you wake-up, fall asleep or at any point of the day for no reason at all

What happens once the signs are recognized? What happens now and better yet, what do you do next? The answers depend on the stage of depression being experienced. At the onset of depression, it may be

14

easier to overcome the challenges it presents. This is primarily because it is the beginning of a bad situation or the trauma is new. In any case, recognition of depression and taking proactive measures to defeat it may be much easier in the beginning.

If you or a loved one is just beginning to feel or exhibit the signs of depression, there are steps you can take immediately. The first step is to take care of yourself or encourage the depressed person to do the same. This doesn't necessarily require a change in medical schedule or for you to work out more often. While both may be necessary, they are not the only things that need to be done. Consider introducing a lifestyle of self-preservation. This allows those dealing with depression to preserve a life of healthiness, happiness and longevity. At this point, you will acknowledge the things you need most to live happily and do what it takes to make them happen. Engage or participate in activities that distract you from things that make you feel sad or anything that promotes a positive approach to a sound mind and puts you at peace each day.

Feelings of depression are more often overcome by connecting with your happy place. This is not necessarily a physical location but sometimes located within. To experience happiness, you may only need to do something that makes you smile or feel great about yourself. The worst part is it's not simple to accomplish, because you may have no idea where to start or what must be done to achieve happiness.

The following activity chart can be helpful in teaching you to separate your day into various feel-good activities.

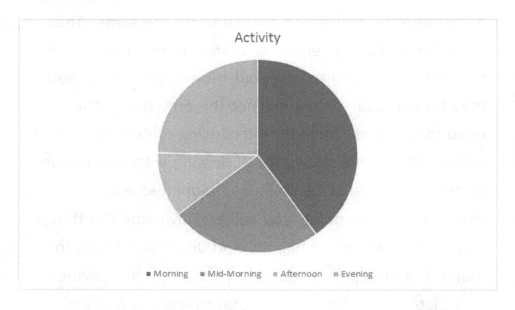

Morning – Morning time will be the most important aspect of your day, as it establishes the climate for the remainder of your day. Once you awake, take a moment to assess your true feelings. Get in touch with them and find out why you have them. Meditate, enjoy a cup of coffee, tea or water. Listen to your favorite music and make a commitment to make the most of whatever the day throws your way. Allow yourself enough time to do yoga or another fun and relaxing exercise. Make mornings all your own by cooking breakfast, juicing or trying a new recipe. Before leaving home, look in the mirror and say out loud at least three things you like about that person staring back at you. Next, say two things out loud that you think you should change about the person staring back at you.

Mid-Morning – Mid-morning is an important time of day for those dealing with depression. This is typically the time you will begin to think of all the things that are going wrong in your life. It's usually this time of day that you encounter others and begin comparing yourself to those around you. STOP! Remember those positive things that you said you admired about yourself before you left home. Don't focus on others and what they are doing but begin to think of ways you can change the things you don't like about yourself. These are the things that matter most but be sure to not pressure yourself. There are 24-hours in a day and what you don't accomplish or change today, you can start again tomorrow.

Afternoon – Afternoons should be used for refuel sessions. Take the time to reenergize or replenish your happiness. Take a stroll through your favorite neighborhood or park. Visit your favorite coffee house or lunch spot. Spend the afternoon reading to kids in a library or local school. These are things or activities that remind you of how much of an essential asset you are in the life of your own and others

Evening – Evening is the best time of day to put your feelings on the shelf. Shut down any negative events that took place during the day. Don't take anything that happened personally and most importantly, don't allow bad situations or occurrences to make you feel less than valuable. Reassess whatever happened during the day and move forward with your evening without dwelling on those times. It may help to tell yourself that you will deal with what you can, when you can. Once the work or school day is over, it's time to just be happy. Schedule an evening out with friends, take in a movie by yourself, attend a concert or enjoy a movie night at home. Long relaxing baths and soothing music are great for ending any kind of day and can help you to relax and sleep better at night.

*Notice that the largest areas of the day are morning and evening. It is because these are the most important times of day for setting and resetting your emotions and feelings. Give these hours considerable time and consideration to help you feel your absolute best each day.

The Stages of Depression

You should try and understand that medical professionals do not acknowledge or assign stages to depression. Keep in mind, the common process of progression that a large category of people identify as stages. Prior to noticing any bodily changes, your thoughts and emotions begin to change. It is common to begin blaming yourself for things that are not your fault or feeling despondent about issues or challenges you are facing in life. Pacing the floor, eating less or not at all and staying up into all hours of the night are common occurrences.

The process or stages as some call them of depression may appear as follows:

Observation – this is the stage where you begin to wonder if depression is the case and what life issues are causing the depression. You begin to observe the changes and identify the symptoms.

Preparation – this stage is where you may speak to someone about the thoughts or feelings you have. You begin to research articles or read self-help guides to see what is happening in your life.

Proactive- this stage begins when you step up and take action. Make an appointment with a health care professional or counselor to seek a professional diagnosis. You may be prescribed medication or begin therapeutic exercises. These measures help to encourage relaxation and relive stress.

How You Feel

Once depression hits, you begin to feel a combination of mixed emotions. You will experience a sense of disconnect from the world, extreme loneliness and a loss of energy or motivation. It helps to communicate or talk to others, forge happy and healthy relationships with your support systems and surround yourself with people or things that make you feel happy and appreciated. These are all positive steps to help battle depression. However, no one expects you to be with someone or depend on others all the time. Therefore, it is imperative that you learn to engage in activities alone without feeling sad or depressed.

Consider the following suggestions to help you enjoy your alone time.

Get Active

Depression can make you feel drained and cause you to lose interest in almost all physical activities. Make a commitment to spend at least thirty minutes per day being active. Ride a bike, throw a ball to your dog in the park, sign-up for a dance class or some other type of physical activity you would enjoy. Professionals suggest that participating in consistent exercises does wonders for your emotional and mental mood. It also helps to alleviate signs of depression that many adults experience. The endorphins that are released during active exercises contribute to mood enhancement and helps to decrease symptoms of depression.

Relax

Most people dealing with depression spend a large part of their day feeling stressed or worried about things beyond their control. It's time to relax. Meditation is a great resource when seeking a relaxed state of mind and body. It disturbs the negative thought pattern.

There are several types of meditation that include traditional and contemporary options. You may consider signing up for a class or if it's more comfortable, follow a meditation expert on television or a YouTube video.

Adopt a Pet

Pets give just as much love as they require. They are great in helping people overcome feelings of depression or loneliness. Caring for a pet will make you feel responsible and in charge. If you have been battling depression, begin with an animal that requires little attention. This will prevent feelings of guilt from settling in if you fail to walk the dog, trim the cat and other responsibilities on a regular schedule. Pets or animals will help bring a sense of fulfillment to your life.

Become a Volunteer

You will find that it feels great to give of your time where others need it most. Become a volunteer in your community, school or at work. Volunteering delivers a feeling of satisfaction and creates structure in an otherwise unorganized lifestyle. You will begin to see how your efforts are needed and appreciated by others, which makes you feel good or better about yourself. You can volunteer as little as two-five hours per month and begin to see the difference in how you feel. It helps to keep it light and not make it feel like an obligation.

Join a Book Club

Do you enjoy reading? Books are a great way to engage your inner happiness. If you prefer to read alone, pick up a motivational or inspirational book. Regardless if you are reading for self-improvement or pleasure. It's critical that you engage in a storyline that shifts your mood and encourages positive emotions.

Turn Up the Music

Do you enjoy music and dancing? Perhaps you have a favorite artist or group that you haven't listened to in a while. Download a few of your favorite songs and listen to them at any time you're feeling down. Dance around to one or more of your favorite songs. It's okay to dance in the park or even in the rain. The point is to turn up the music, nod your head or dance the night away.

How Depression Impacts Your Body

Depression can alter your physical composition, just as it does your emotional state. Long before it becomes too bad, your body may begin to exhibit signs that it is being impacted by depression. Signs may exist temporarily or long-term as the result of a traumatic experience. If you have been experiencing prolonged feelings of sadness for longer than two or three weeks, it could be a sign of severe depression. Other conditions associated with the signs that present themselves during depression are Post-Traumatic Stress Disorder (PTSD) or bipolar disorder.

Depression is diagnosed in a person that exhibits five or more of these signs for two or more consecutive weeks.

Mood is sad or feeling defeated most days	Tired or exhaustion without reason
Unable to enjoy favorite activities	Excessive or lack of sleep
Extreme weight loss	Extreme weight gain
Diminished self-worth	Having a hard time completing tasks
Lingering thoughts of suicide	Isolation from others are being withdrawn

You should know that depression impacts not only your life, but the life of those around you as well. It can begin to cause changes in important relationships at home, work, and in your social circle. How has depression caused your life to change? Maybe changes have occurred and you're not aware that depression is the cause.

Sufferers of depression may also experience the following impacts on their body.

If you or someone you know has begun to experience unexplainable feelings, emotions and changes within the human physique, depression could be the cause. It is important to seek help before these conditions lead to more severe, life-threatening episodes. The way your body reacts to your emotions has a huge impact on its performance. Take the initiative to undergo regular mental and physical check-ups to sustain your happiness and well-being.

Chapter 2 Understanding Brain Chemistry

Human motivation is the innate source that drives proactive, goal-oriented and action-taking behaviors, which can be emotional, environmental, and biological in essence. The biological and cognitive roots of motivation are strongly triggered in the limbic system of the brain, where activation takes place within a bundle of axons that travel through the hypothalamus area. This system is stimulated by various elements such as chemical administration (through food, supplements, and medications), electrical stimulation and the existing or genetic balance of the brain chemistry that affects overall mental functioning.

Neurotransmitters are the chemical substances and messengers in the human brain that influence synaptic activity. The widely known groups of neurotransmitters include Serotonin, GABA, Endorphins and Catecholamines, which are responsible for mood regulation, sleep, pleasure, energy, focus, motivation and the ability to perform tasks. Each of them works in synchrony with each other. Any imbalance will cause deficiencies that can make anyone depressed, tired, irritable, anxious and inattentive while the excess can lead to risks of abnormal functioning and perception.

The Catecholamines group includes Dopamine, as well as Epinephrine (Adrenaline) and Norepinephrine (Noradrenaline), which are mainly centered on energy, stress management, focus and motivation. They influence the inclination to take action and persevere, either towards attaining something desirable or avoiding something unwanted. This neurotransmitter group influences the drive to perform with enthusiasm, as well as producing feelings of arousal, which is a combination that strengthens motivation.

The strong connection between pleasure and motivation enables the brain to drive one towards tasks that are perceived as approved, good or right. Dopamine signals, for instance, predict the reward of a specific task. In moments of stress, they encourage the performance of needed tasks that obtain desirable achievements, and also discourage against wrong or unattainable tasks. The pathways of motivation within the brain are generally complex, but with safe and proper excitation this motivational system can have rewarding and pleasurable effects, such as having a stronger desire to be proactive, increased energy, and a feeling of cordiality.

Chapter 3 The Difference Between Normal Anxiety and Chronic Anxiety Disorder

The United States Department of Health and Human Services (HHS) identifies five types of anxiety disorders: GAD, SAD, OCD, Panic, and PTSD. These are not mutually exclusive. Unfortunately, people can have one or more or all of these disorders simultaneously.

GAD, or Generalized Anxiety Disorder, is when anxiety becomes a way of life, and the person is more often than not worried, nervous, and cannot seem to focus on the tasks at hand. In fact, when a person experiencing GAD is at peace and happy, they're glad about it, but at the same time, they wonder why. It's normal to be concerned about finances, or family or work issues, but there is a cycle of worry that can be uncontrollable. If left untreated, this constant apprehension causes emotional distress and can have severe negative effects on relationships at home or work.

GAD can affect people of all ages but is most common from childhood to middle age, sometimes along with irritability, insomnia, restlessness, and in extreme cases, suicidal thoughts. The more the worry, the more undesired physical symptoms emerge, such as headaches, nausea, stomachaches, and sweating.

In the United States alone, it is reported that over three million each year suffer from GAD. The number is most likely much higher because so many don't report their issue. Many with mild forms of anxiety have learned to manage it and live what on the outside seems to be a wonderful life. Left untreated, this could progress to it being hard to just perform regular activities of daily life.

If believing the worst will definitely happen becomes a way of life for you, and you expect the worst to happen each and every time, there are grounds for pause. If there is no obvious reason for the concern, and it lasts for six months or more, it is time to take action. With GAD, you experience the sense of nearby danger when there is none.

SAD, or Social Anxiety Disorder, is common in its mildest form. Many have experienced when in school having to give a presentation in front of the class - the heart races, and nerves kick in so much the palms sweat, teeth chatter, and knees start to shake. Someone with this disorder experiences this reaction every time they're in a crowd of people, or any type of gathering or activity that others would see as normal or fun. Feelings of embarrassment or humiliation are constant, as are feelings that you might offend someone, or even worse, be rejected by someone.

Kids may not want to go to school. Adults may not want to go to work. Feeling awkward and self-conscious, limiting eye contact, speaking in a quiet voice that is hard for people to hear, and avoiding attention at all costs, are all signs that SAD may be an issue in your life. Epidemiological research shows that SAD is the third most prevalent psychological disorder in the United States, with depression coming in at number one, and alcoholism at number two.

Usually, when sufferers of SAD are in social situations, extreme anxiety occurs, that is effectively eliminated by withdrawal from the social environment, and complete removal from the situation. However, withdrawal and isolation are never a good remedy, as it can contribute to depression, and thus, the circle continues.

OCD, or Obsessive-Compulsive Disorder, is the type of anxiety that was affectionately mimicked in the television character Adrian Monk on the USA Network series "Monk". Adrian lived with particular obsessions, such as not wanting to touch anyone, and repeatedly sanitizing his hands due to an exaggerated fear of germs. He also had urges to correct anything that is not in perfect order or harmony, such as an uneven number of items, even when it caused embarrassment. Other examples of this: someone constantly checking the stove to make sure they turned it off, or the door to make sure they locked it. Or it could be becoming "antsy" or frustrated with any items not perfectly straight or categorized, or having to perform daily activity in a different order than usual, like putting socks and shoes on before combing hair.

The two main symptoms of OCD are compulsions and obsessions, but they are not mutually exclusive. Compulsions are when, like Monk, a person has a constant need to think about and act on the need for cleanliness, checking on the status of things like door locks and the stove being turned off, keeping or rearranging things in a particular order, and constantly washing hands. This behavior might compel them to spend one or two hours a day focusing on these needs, even if it causes delays or frustration. Completing these rituals only gives a temporary sense of peace or relief. When these rituals are not able to be completed, the anxiety dramatically increases.

Obsessions are thoughts about issues that keep repeating and cause anxiety, such as unwanted pornography addiction, fear of contamination by germs, or doing or having things in perfect order. Some also have tics, like clearing of the throat, unusual blinking of the eye, shrugging the shoulders, grunting or sniffing.

 People with OCD know they have a problem, so they do their best to avoid people or situations that may be triggers. It has been noted that if a person has experienced abuse as a child, they are at a higher risk of OCD.

Panic Disorder is the type of disorder as described earlier with the example of a downhill bike ride with no brakes - sudden and unexpected episodes of a sudden and intense fear of an impending bad physical event, such as a heart attack. These sudden attacks happen when there is no danger present at all. They can take place at any location, in any environment, at any time, and with no prior warning. Without the proper knowledge, this may end up in a trip to the emergency room, with thoughts of certain cardiac stress, but ending up with a non-diagnosis.

Some of the symptoms include dizziness, rapid heartbeats or skipping beats, a feeling like choking, tightness of the chest, tingling of extremities, abdominal issues, and an overall feeling of impending doom or death. These are also symptoms of "real" cardiac issues, so it's only after a barrage of expensive testing, with a clean bill of physical health, that it's properly diagnosed. If not diagnosed, the person may have a fear of losing their mind or going crazy when they realize it's all in their mind. Without proper treatment, the stress of this disorder may lead to physical symptoms such as constipation or diarrhea, IBS, or chronic fatigue.

The emotional consequences of this disorder are numerous, including the inability to drive, the fear of being left alone, and basic daily activities. Life is turned upside down, and there is a sense of basic powerlessness and hopelessness that can lead to depression and a generally poorer existence. For panic disorder suffers, to function "normally" in life would be a gift. Women tend to worry more than men about the physical symptoms brought about by a panic attack, and men tend to worry more about the social consequences.

This condition can be brought on as a consequence of burning the candle at both ends for a long period of time, without giving the body and mind time to rest, rejuvenate and repair. It's also possible that it is genetic, but there are conflicting studies about this.

PTSD, or Post Traumatic Stress Disorder, is more well-known than the others and is sometimes identified as TSRD, or Trauma- and Stressor-Related Disorder. We've all heard the stories of brave men and women who've fought the good fight for their country, facing the possibility of death every single day, and constantly witnessing the utterly gruesome maiming and death of comrades in action. When troops return home from combat, things just aren't the same, and it's hard to assimilate back into the normal routine, as a constant recollection of these violent and emotionally draining acts affects their day to day living.

PTSD can also be caused by violent crimes such as rape or mugging, after natural disasters like experiencing a hurricane or tornado, or any type of horrific accident where violence occurred and life was threatened. Often those with PTSD experience vivid nightmares or flashbacks where they relive the terrible moments over and over again. Flashbacks could be triggered by anything that reminds them of the event. Sufferers may blame themselves for the event, or even for surviving the event if they were one of the few who did make it through.

Symptoms include insomnia, outbursts of anger, difficulty showing affection, always being on edge and tense, and startling easily. Physical symptoms are similar to Panic Disorder symptoms and include nausea, muscle tension, high blood pressure, rapid heart rate, and diarrhea.

While this is a commonly known issue with those who have experienced combat, it can also occur with children who have suffered physical abuse, or who grew up in dangerous situations.

Chapter 4 What You Can Do About It?

Breathing is characterized as a programmed capacity of the body that is overseen by the respiratory framework and ran by the central nervous system. Breathing can be seen as a reaction of the body when it is faced with pressure, where there is a stamped change in the breathing tempo and rates.

This is a piece of the body's fight or flight system and is a piece of the body's reaction to upsetting circumstances. People have been enabled to control their breathing patterns, and studies have proven that with our capacity to control our breathing patterns we can oversee and battle pressure and other wellbeing related conditions such as depression and anxiety.

Controlled breathing when utilized in the act of yoga, tai chi and other reflection exercises, is likewise used to achieve a condition of unwinding. Controlled breathing strategies can mitigate the accompanying conditions:

• Anxiety issues

- Panic attacks

- Chronic fatigue disorder

- Asthma assaults

- Severe agony

- High pulse

- Insomnia

- Stress

Stress and Breathing

The key job of breathing is to carry oxygen into the body and expel carbon dioxide from the body through the lungs. The muscles that encompass the lungs, similar to the stomach, control the motion of the lungs, just as the muscles that are found between the ribs.

An individual who encounters stress changes their patterns of breathing. Typically, when you are on edge, you make little, shallower breaths with the utilization of your shoulder muscles, rather than with the muscles in your stomach, so as to control the breathing conduct in the lungs.

This sort of breathing intrudes on the gas ratio in the body. Then again, hyperventilation or shallow over-breathing can incredibly drag out the feeling of anxiety as it triggers the side effects of the worry to exacerbate.

The Breath-Relaxation Response

On the off chance that you are feeling unfocused or restless, you can loosen up your body by breathing gradually and tenderly through the nose to help even out your breathing patterns. Following the breathing example of a loosened-up individual can quiet the sensory system that deals with the automatic elements of the body.

Controlled breathing can likewise change the physiological condition of the individual, which incorporates, diminishing the pulse, bringing down stress hormones, diminishing lactic corrosive development in the tissues of the muscles, and managing the oxygen and carbon dioxide levels in the circulatory system.

Parasympathetic versus Sympathetic Nervous System

Instances of deep breathing empower the Parasympathetic nervous system, or PNS, which is in charge of the bodily exercises when in a casual chilled out state or when you are very still. On the other hand, hyperventilation supports the inverse.

The Sympathetic Nervous System, or SNS, is in charge of the physical exercises that are identified with the fight or flight reaction in the body when stress is identified. You can look at these two frameworks like this; PNS is the quiet sister, and SNS is the insane, non-thoughtful sister that is continuously very close to a mental meltdown.

With regards to the elements of our body, the one in particular that we can promptly control is our breathing, which is the means by which we can recuperate our bodies. By changing your breathing patterns, you can help different pieces of your body work regularly to avert the genuine reactions to stressors.

Breathing Exercises for Anxiety Reduction

There are three deep breathing activities that you can practice helping you beat depression and anxiety. As mentioned before, the action of hyperventilating can extraordinarily intensify stress and anxiety. The accompanying relaxing activities can be utilized anyplace to enable you to decrease the side effects of anxiety and stress.

Coherent Breathing

This controlled breathing activity gets you to reduce your breathing speed drastically and boosts the heart rate variability or on the other hand HRV, which is an element of the Parasympathetic Nervous System.

The strategy is straightforward and can be performed anyplace. Begin by taking a full breath in, while counting to five and after that count to five again as you breathe out. The method has you breathing at a rate of five breaths per minute.

Observe how the adjustments in your breathing influence the HRV, which is in charge of exchanging your sensory system structure the PNS to the SNS, or vice versa. What it comes down to is the higher HRV implies a more advantageous cardiovascular framework and more grounded reaction to stressors.

Resistance Breathing

Resistance breathing, as its name infers, is breathing with resistance in the progression of air all through the body. It is a way of breathing where you restricted the pathway of air or use items, such as a straw, through which inhaling and exhaling happen. A simpler method to achieve this is to inhale through your nose instead of your mouth.

Another way you can rehearse resistance breathing is by relaxing through the course of reciting or singing. This is a viable way to achieve this activity on the grounds that the vocal cords adequately thin down the air's pathway.

Breath Moving

Breath moving is the method in which you imagine yourself breathing. It causes you to inhale like you are driving oxygen to the highest point of your head and flushing out all the carbon dioxide from your body. As you are doing this, you have to envision that you are moving your breath from your lungs to the highest point of your head.

Figuring out how to control your breathing can drastically lessen your side effects of pressure and help you to defeat your anxiety disorder. Consolidating controlled breathing methods, similar to the ones recorded above, with mindfulness, can keep your mind quiet and what's more, centered around the present.

How to Control Your Thinking to Control Anxiety

On the off chance that you regularly experience odd and insane considerations that are exasperating and want to get these musings out of your head, at that point you'll be glad to realize that you can do that when you learn the most effective method to deal with your contemplations to enable you to control your anxiety.

While it isn't unexpected to have insane and bizarre contemplations from time to time, what makes it not typical and strange, is when they reoccur regularly and when you experience issues overlooking them.

These insane musings can even lead to dread in light of the fact that the thought is so irritating in nature. On the off chance that you need to have the option to deal with your considerations, you'll have to comprehend the facts that encompass these thoughts, their underlying foundations, and how to maintain a strategic distance from them.

Deal with Your Anxiety by Managing Your Thoughts

When you are encountering insane contemplations, you are encountering anxious thoughts. An individual who doesn't experience the ill effects of anxiety will experience issues understanding the different ways that anxiety can influence the body and the psyche.

The legitimate explanation to this is all individuals experience anxiety at various occasions during their life. Some normal encounters that can bring on anxiety are before a job interview, test, or asking someone out.

Be that as it may, these examples of anxiety tend to pass directly after the conclusion of the occasion. All things considered, individuals who experience anxiety disorder are entirely different from the regular anxiety others experience.

Anxiety disorder can have an effect on both the physical and emotional parts of an actual existence, which can prompt a noteworthy lopsidedness. The production of insane and terrifying thoughts is one of the essential side effects that individuals with anxiety experience and deal with.

Anxiety has the ability to change one's thinking and make you think, and accept, that you are getting out of touch with the real world. It makes you believe that you are losing your mind and, in this way, going insane.

In the event that you are experiencing these side effects, you don't have to stress over it, what's more, they are only the impacts of your anxious considerations.

How do Anxious Thoughts Begin?

There are distinctive anxious thoughts that might be considered insane. These contemplations are established in worry, however, the vast majority of them are established in the anxiety symptoms that you might be enduring.

Undesirable Images

Individuals who experience the ill effects of obsessive-compulsive disorder, OCD, are the ones that regularly experience undesirable images. These undesirable images are typically framed by their sentiments of stress, uncertainty, and the need to ensure their lives and those they care about.

Now and then these undesirable images can be activated by what they dread the most. For instance, the individuals who experience the ill effects of OCD may envision some type of serious brutality, which can be incredibly upsetting. In light of this pain, they lock the majority of the doors.

Or on the other hand, they may envision an extreme fire that may occur, so they consistently check to see if the gas is leaking. These activities are legitimately connected to their anxiety.

Unwarranted Worries

Worry is the foundation of anxiety. In this way, somebody who experiences anxiety encounters unusual stresses, which are frequently unreasonable. It makes them worry that something terrible may occur. The stressing side effect can be amazingly persistent and subjective, be that as it may, everything comes down to the anxiety sufferer getting a peculiar feeling, which makes them uneasy.

The Fear of Losing Your Mind

The genuine fear that anxiety-ridden people are going insane comes from the side effects of anxiety being so vivid to the point that they may really think they are going crazy and losing it. The particular feel of anxiety can make your head turn with numerous bothersome and fast contemplations that are amazingly difficult to control.

This fear can be irrational to the point that it influences everyday exercises and can tremendously affect the life of those with an anxiety issue.

The Most Effective Method to Avoid Anxious Thoughts

Anxiety is influenced by your thinking, and your thinking is influenced by anxiety. With one compounding on the other, the circumstance can turn out to be very difficult to control. Here are a few different ways that you can begin to maintain a strategic distance from anxious thinking and end the cycle of worrying.

See the Thought for What it is

You would prefer not to think about the certain idea because fear that accompanies it. Regardless of how insane the idea you are having is, the point at which you learn and practice to confront it, the thoughts can never again be a reason to be afraid of the thought, and it doesn't make a difference if that particular idea reoccurs.

Create the Thought Yourself

Another way that you can deal with your thoughts is by creating them before they even occur. At the point when your brain is accustomed to the thought, your fear will be stifled.

Put the Thoughts on Paper

One way that experts have those experiencing anxiety manage their feelings of trepidation is to record the upsetting thoughts as an approach to get it out of the head. When somebody has restless thoughts, recording those on a bit of paper resembles setting it someplace where they remain permanent, which enables the brain to unwind and not to have to worry about it further.

This routine of recording dreadful and restless thoughts tends to conciliate the psyche and enables it to overlook those thoughts in the long run. These are only a couple of the simple methods that you can start doing to manage anxious thoughts that show up arbitrarily. While you will, in any case, need to manage your fundamental anxiety, these straightforward advances can help you stop the incapacitating thoughts dead in their tracks.

Chapter 5 How to Use CBT for Depression

The process of CBT therapy is pretty simple. Basically, a therapist assists you in recognizing false beliefs you have about yourself and your environment and replaces them with healthier options that accurately reflect reality. For example, you could have some thoughts of hopelessness or unworthiness and you believe that life is out to "get" you. Or you might be obsessed with your shortcomings and unable to see anything good about yourself.

CBT brings your awareness of these issues to the surface. It makes you confront those demons and deal with them head-on. Once you're in the habit of bringing to light negative issues and dealing with them, CBT then teaches you how to switch out the negative, destructive thoughts for more empowering, positive ones. As your attitude changes, so does your behavior. This subtle shift can improve your depression symptoms.

To illustrate, maybe you've been conditioned to think only of negative thoughts about yourself. CBT will help you immediately rewire those negative thought.

A perfect example of this would be to consider any phobias you may have. How have those phobias influenced your behavior and your choices? What's unfortunate is that what we fear limits us. If you have a fear of insects, it isn't likely that we'll spot you outside in the jungles of the Amazon hiking. If you have a fear of flying, you're probably going to travel mostly by car, right?

In many cases, this fear can become debilitating and limit our quality of life. For that reason, we might want to work with someone to get over this paralyzing fear. They want to be able to push past their fear and regain full quality of life.

It's for this reason that people seek therapy. They want help from a professional who has the answer to help them release their fears. One of the ways of working with anxiety including depression is cognitive behavioral therapy.

Continuous practice of the CBT process will slowly guide you to a better quality of life. Sometimes it takes a while but you will start to feel better and eventually get on with your life. However, this takes consistent effort on a daily basis to improve. It's not a magic pill or something that you can do once and you're cured forever. With most things, it takes consistent actions.

Managing Depression With CBT

People thrive in environments that help them meet their innate social needs. As human beings, we had these innate needs. We have an insatiable desire to fulfill them. And when we don't fulfill them we unavoidably suffer. It's reassuring to let sufferers know that it isn't just about what they have inside their minds but it also has something to do with the extent to which their environment helps meets their needs. It is important to take action to identify and meet these needs. For people who meet their needs, they are less likely to suffer from depression or anxiety.

Anxiety is a signal that you're not meeting your needs in some way. The way we feel isn't just a response to the way things are in the world but it's also how we make sense of them. Strong emotions arise as an afterthought because thoughts occur you can feel them. It is often easier and more powerful to change feelings that it is to change thoughts.

This Neuroscience contradicts traditional CBT.

Clinical hypnosis is the best way to change thoughts. So for phobias and post-traumatic stress disorder, it's not faulty thinking that is the issue and the chance for making significant progress alone with CBT are remote, but not completely condemning it altogether. It can be useful in less traumatic conditions.

Actions, thoughts, and emotions are all connected to mental health. We call this the mental health wheel. As we make changes in one area of the wheel, the other areas will change as well. We can change our emotions and feel better by making changes in one of the other areas.

Generally, thoughts and actions are conducive to changes. Therefore, cognitive behavioral therapy will focus on changing these two areas.

Ronald is 62 years old who lives alone. Since his wife, Rita died three years ago; he's been committed to volunteering at his local community. He greets people at the door and organizes the weekly bingo event every week. Ronald feels a sense of reward by volunteering but also enjoys the social interactions he feels with other adults in his community. In fact, Ronald has made a few good friends. They play Bingo talk on the phone and talk regularly.

Six weeks ago Ronald broke his hip after falling on his way to the community center. Ronald had surgery and spent three weeks in the hospital. Before his discharge, the doctor told Ronald that it might take about a year for him to fully heal. Ronald has been recovering well but develops this fear that he'll fall again so he stopped volunteering at the community center. He has lost interest in his friends and playing games that he stays in bed almost all day.

Ronald is exhibiting symptoms of depression. Ronald starts to feel sad and hopeless. He thinks that maybe things won't get better for him. He doesn't want to be a burden but he feels useless and doesn't want to bother his friends and he stopped calling them. He lost his social support which adds to his feelings of being depressed. Based on Ronald's thoughts, emotions, health, and actions, Ronald might be suffering from mild depression.

Let's analyze Ronald situation. His thoughts could be like this: "All of my friends have forgotten me and since my wife is gone, I'm bound to be alone forever."

Thoughts impact his emotions and he feels sad and hopeless. These negative emotions further affect his actions which made him stay in bed and stop calling his friends. His actions impact his health as well. Staying in bed delays his hip rehabilitation. By refraining himself from socializing, it makes his depression worse. Therefore, thoughts, emotions, and actions all connected to each other which affect not only your mental health but also your total well-being.

By targeting Ronald's thoughts and actions CBT can help him with his depression. Let's see how Ronald can use CBT to stop the depression train in its track.

One day Ronald starts to feel hopeless about his recovery from surgery. He learned through one of his CBT therapy sessions that when he feels down he should engage himself in an enjoyable activity. Ronald decides to call up one of his friends from the community center. This is a positive action. His friend answers the phone and says, "Ronald it's so nice to hear from you.

All of us in the community center were worried about you."

Ronald was relieved to hear that his friends have not forgotten about him. This impacts his thoughts and Ronald believes that he's not alone after all. Ronald thoughts impact his emotions. Thinking about his friends and realize he's not alone makes him happy. Ronald emotions help improve his health. Now, he is motivated to see his friends in the community center again. He works hard to improve his health so he can get back to his friends. Ronald was able to identify actions that helped him stop the depression train in its tracks. With practice and help of a therapist, Ronald begins to feel less depressed over time and make better decisions about how to care for himself.

CBT methods confront irrational beliefs, requiring them to be analyzed for their validity. For example, if a person is terrified to cross the road because they think they're going to get hit by a car, the therapist might ask that person how often people get run over within a year. You might discover that it's a very small population and that the sphere is bigger than the reality. This is what we called disputing irrational beliefs. The more you cross the road and see that you are unlikely to get run over by a car, the more confident you are that it's less likely to happen and what you used to believe was faulty. However, you have to be willing to participate in the therapy in order for it to work. If you are unwilling to cross the road at all, you'll never know that it's safe to do so.

Crossing the road is an example of doing the homework required in therapy. The therapist can lead you to new ideas but it's your responsibility to challenge those ideas by doing the exercises your therapist is giving you. You can't just talk your way out of fear. You have to experience the sphere under actual stimulus in order to confront and overcome depressing thoughts. That doesn't mean that you have to start off at the highest level of fear or in this case crossing the road. Maybe you start with crossing the street in front of your house or crossing smaller roads or your driveway. Then you can build up to something bigger.

Who Can Benefit From CBT?

Any individual experiencing mild to moderate depression can benefit from Cognitive Behavioral Therapy even in the absence of medication. There are research studies suggesting that a combination treatment of CBT and medication can be an effective treatment for major depression. CBT is also shown to reduce relapses in patients experiencing frequent relapses after being through other treatments.

CBT is not only useful for people with a mental health disorder. It can likewise benefit those who want to learn how to manage effectively stress which continuously bombards us from all directions.

While there are other treatments available for cognitive behavioral issues, CBT is often preferred by many psychotherapists as it can quickly help them identify and cope with specific issues and challenges. Basically, CBT requires a fewer number of sessions compares to other types of behavioral therapy and done in a structured way. CBT is used as an effective tool to address emotional issues and help you with the following:

- Cope with grief over the loss of someone dear to you

- Overcome emotional trauma as a result of violence or abuse

- Manage symptoms of mental illness and prevent relapses

- Learn skills and techniques on coping with life's crisis

- Resolve conflicts related to relationship issues and learn to improve ways of communicating

- Cope with a medical condition

- Manage chronic physical symptoms of cognitive behavioral disorders

- Treat mental illness when medication treatment is not a good option

- Determine ways to manage and control emotions

Although CBT is a stand-alone treatment, in some cases, it can be more effective when combined with medication treatment such as the use of antidepressants.

Risk Involve in CBT

There is minimal risk involved in having cognitive behavioral therapy. While it definitely explores emotions and experiences which could, at times, provide discomfort, this feeling is sure not to last long as you become more adjusted to the method used in the treatment. You may cry, get angry or upset when undergoing sessions or may leave you physically and mentally drained.

In some forms of CBT like in Exposure Therapy, you may be required to confront a situation that you may want to avoid in real life such as walking along the sidewalks when you are afraid of being crushed by an uncontrolled vehicle. You may experience stress and temporary anxiety while being subjected to such challenging situations. However, if your therapist is skillful, risks are minimized and you will be acquiring coping skills which will help you overcome negative emotions like fear.

Preparation for CBT

If you decide to try Cognitive Behavioral Therapy, here's how to get started.

Look for a therapist. If you have enough time to browse through the internet, you can find one nearest to your location. You may also get some referral from a friend, a doctor, or other trusted sources.

Consider the cost. Talk with the therapist about feed and payment options. If you have health coverage plans, find out its coverage as some coverage only includes a certain number of sessions in a year.

Reassess your concerns.

Before you start a collaboration effort with your therapist, you must have definite concerns to work on. By providing a definite starting point to work on, you and your therapist could be saving some time and you could be saving money.

Checking a Therapist Qualifications

Before deciding to pick out a therapist, here are some factors you need to consider in your selection.

Background and Education – Depending on their education and rile, a trained psychologist can have a number of job titles. A majority of them have a master's or doctorate degree in psychology and counseling. Medical doctors specializing in mental health or psychiatrists can provide psychotherapy and prescribe medications.

Areas of Expertise – Make sure that the therapist has adequate experience CBT treatment particularly in your areas of concern.

The key is to find a therapist who is skillful and experience in conducting CBT to match your need.

What Can You Expect?

Cognitive Behavioral Therapy session can be conducted one-on-one, in groups, or with family. It can also be done with other people with similar issues. Activities can include:

Awareness of your mental health condition

Learning, applying, and practicing techniques like cooping, relaxation, stress management, resilience, and assertiveness.

In Your Initial Therapy

At the start, expect your therapist to delve deeper into your background and history including your experiences, emotions, views, and opinions on certain matters related to your areas of concern. It is the aim of the therapist to determine the underlying reason for your concerned behavior. While your therapist is evaluating your behavior and relating provided information on the issue, this can also be a good opportunity for you to know your therapist as well and see if you are a good match. Make sure that you are able to gain a good understanding of the following:

- The goal of your treatment
- What approach will your therapist adopt for the treatment?
- What options for treatment do you have?
- How long is each session
- Target duration for the therapy

Note, though, that it may take a number of sessions before your therapist will have a full grasp on your concern or situation to be able to determine the best course of action to take. If you aren't comfortable with the therapist, try choosing someone else as it is important that you can work comfortably with your therapist to make it successful.

When CBT is Ongoing

You will be encouraged to talk more about yourself and the issue that is troubling you. It might be hard for you do fully reveal your inner thoughts and feelings but if your therapist is skillful enough, it would not be difficult for him or her to coach you in opening up.

CBT is focused on a specific problem concentration on the achievement of the goal you both have set up. So while the therapy is ongoing, you will be asked to do some tasks at home to apply what you have learned and discovered from the session.

The approach will depend on your specific situation and preferences as there is no one solution for all problems in CBT.

Length of Therapy

Generally, CBT is considered a short-term therapy but you may need to discuss this with your therapist. Here are some factors that affect the length of the therapy.

- The severity of your symptoms

- The type of disorder

- How long had you spotted the symptoms prior to your first check up

- How much stress you are currently experiencing

- How quickly is your progress

- How much support you have from your family and other people

- Availability of funds to support the therapy

Confidentiality

CBT is confidential in nature unless there is an immediate threat to security or when existing law governs that it needs to be reported to concerned authorities. Situations under these circumstances include:

- An immediate threat to harm yourself
- An immediate threat to other people
- Abuse of other people (child or vulnerable adults)
- Inability to safeguard yourself

Possibilities

There is always a possibility that Cognitive Behavioral Therapy may not be able to solve your behavioral issue. However, you can learn many things out of it such as the skill to cope with your situation in a healthy way making it possible for you to enjoy life and feel better and happier.

Getting the Most Out of CBT

Cognitive Behavioral Therapy is not for everyone. There are cases with minimal results but if you want to maximize results, you can take some steps to get the most out of your therapy.

Consider Your Therapist as Your Partner

The therapy can be most effective when you are contributing and sharing in the decision making. Remember that this is collaborative and not just a one-way process. Make sure that you and your therapist are in agreement about issues and how to resolve them. Together the two of you must work for hand in hand you set goals to achieve and assess progress from time to time.

Open Up and Be Honest

Your willingness to open up and be honest about everything is the key to CBT's success. Since the method involves your willingness to share your experiences, emotions, and behavior while being open to new discoveries, insights, and solutions, any reluctance to open up everything to your therapist because of shame, pain, or fear of their reaction will hamper the flow of the therapy and may end up to it being unsuccessful and ineffective. So if you have any reservations, let your therapist know about it.

Be Consistent

There are times when skipping therapy sessions may prove to be tempting. Remember, however, that doing so can disrupt your progress. Do your best to attend all sessions and give some thoughts on things you want to tackle with your therapist.

CHAPTER 6 Types of Depression

Depression occurs in diverse, which means it occurs in very many ways. Being anxious or having unstable emotions are some of the renowned personality disorders. Imagine the emotional impact one gets after watching your loved one feeling depressed.it is, therefore, a hurtful situation. The consequences are destructive, which can even result in the individual committing suicide.

For a proper treatment of such victims, it is wise to know the type of depression one is experiencing. It is advisable to visit a clinic as soon as you realize you are experiencing some sorrows disorders. Visit the therapist as early as possible because depression is manageable at an early stage. When it is at its late-stage, it develops to become a chronic condition that puts one under pressure of health complication. Recognizing the type of depression, you are suffering from is essential because the psychiatrist will know the kind of therapeutically program to put you through. The following are some of the types of this illness.

The first type is major depressive disorder. It is the commonly known type of depression because it affects many people in society. It exhibits the typical symptoms that are accustomed to stressful reactions. These emotions involve the feeling of sadness, hopelessness, emptiness, low self-esteem, and loss of interest in major recreational activities. These symptoms are easily recognizable to a patient, and one should seek medical attention as early as possible. This disorder falls under two main categories, which are atypical depression and, melancholic type. The atypical ones always anxious therefore they eat and sleep a lot, and the melancholic beings tend to suffer from insomnia and guiltiness

There is this type of stress which is resistant the antidepressant drugs. This kind of condition is referred to as the treatment of resistant depression. You can administer any medications to this patient, but still, they are not working. They always have unknown causes where their most prominent suspects are the genetic, or environmental causatives. For one to treat those victims, psychotherapy is recommended for one to assess the reason for that moody feeling. You may also administer different types of antidepressants to establish the medicine that heals that person.

Other people who are not healed quickly from significant depression experience the subsyndromal condition. This menace involves one experiencing many melancholic disorders. In simple one is engrossed with different symptoms showing varying characteristics. You may experience melancholic and at the same time, atypical illness. The physician must be quick to detect this condition because if the patient is affected by many sicknesses, chances of healing are less.

The persistent depressive disorder involves a state of stubborn symptoms. What does it mean by them being stubborn? It means that the syndrome is continuous over time. The syndromes seem to restructure themselves where if one sign is treated, it changes and reforms to terminal disorder. Such complications involve sleeping problems, fatigue, loss of appetite, and many other conditions. The best thing for a psychiatrist to diagnose such a patient is by combining both psychotherapy and medicinal diagnosis.

Depression due to diseases is another type. Some of the chronic illnesses cause stigma to the victims. Think of how you would react if tested HIV positive, cancer, or any other fatal diseases. 'I will kill myself,' 'everybody will laugh at me and despise me.' These are your probable thoughts you would experience if told the bad news. Feelings of loneliness, regret, and guiltiness will eat you strike on you like a hungry lion.

Substance intake depression is a major one attributed to the intoxicants. Intoxication comes from people indulging in drugs and alcohol. The results were those people hallucinating or do unusual things. They will, therefore, find other people do not agree to those deeds, hence feel emotionally discouraged. Some end up in crimes and theft to buy those drugs. These substances change your mood, loss of concern on pleasurable practices, and feeling empty always. Specialized rehabs centers are useful in healing those patients.

It is every parent's joy to have a baby. However, did you know that for some people, child giving can be stressful? Probably this amazes you, but it is a fact. Some mothers change their attitude after giving birth because there is a change in hormones, fatigue, or fear of raising a child. Fathers, in their part, can change their mood when they feel their workload will be increased. Consequently, some folks become stressful.

Chapter 7 Mindfulness and CBT

A term you may have heard about in relation to CBT is "Mindfulness." So, what is it? Developed for individuals who suffer from frequent, recurring, and often severe depressions, Mindfulness combines CBT techniques with breathing exercises, meditation, visualization, and other such techniques that can empower one to move past stress and back into more productive modes of thinking.

Basic Principles

Mindfulness requires you to stop ruminating in the past and worrying about the future. When you are feeling anxious, you know that you can't just stop. When it comes to Mindfulness, the aim is to help you reduce your momentary anxiety by grounding you in the present moment.

Mindfulness techniques are methods to pull your thoughts from the rumination over past events you can no longer control. Whenever you are thinking of something embarrassing that happened, or maybe an event that you are worried will sneak back up on you, it can keep you from enjoying the moment.

Similarly, if you are always stressed about the future, then you will start to lose yourself in the present moment, and sometimes other people will notice that you are not all there. Thinking about the future doesn't always involve negative thoughts. You may fantasize about a life that's seemingly unachievable, one with fancy houses, money, and more friends and family to provide comfort. Though these thoughts don't necessarily cause anxiety, they can lead to depression when avoiding current problems by fantasizing about a future that may never come.

Mindfulness involves any activity that is going to pull you from these moments and bring you to the present— a time that matters most. These types of fantasies and rumination patterns are forms of dissociation.

Disassociation can be debilitating. You may find yourself so stuck in bed that you can't move. Other times, it can affect your memory.

How Mindfulness is Connected to CBT

Since CBT is about rewiring your brain, Mindfulness will help give you a way to stop unrealistic fantasies before they get started. Instead of giving into a thought, a

Mindfulness technique will help you bring yourself back to the present.

Sometimes one starts to disassociate because they don't want to confront a certain issue. If you are triggered by something or someone, you might mentally remove yourself from the situation and think of something else. This adjustment in thought may help temporarily, but you are still not managing your root issues. You should know how to use CBT Mindfulness techniques to better prepare you for these attempts at disassociation.

How Mindfulness Can Help

Have you ever sat through a class and thought, "I need to pay attention. I need to focus." Then, an hour later, the class has ended, and you realize you fantasized about what you were going to do over the weekend or maybe pictured yourself on a trip in a tropical area. Instead of paying attention to class, your mind was in a different state, so when you attempt to study, it is more challenging than it would have been if you had paid attention.

Mindfulness will help pull you back to the classroom. Sometimes we know what it takes to pay attention, but we don't always catch ourselves when we start daydreaming. You don't always recognize that you are disassociating until after the fact when you ask yourself where you are or what happened in the past few minutes. When we disassociate too often, negative side effects will emerge including anxiety, confusion, and memory loss.

Mindfulness

Mindfulness is similar to meditation, but it doesn't have to be practiced in the same way. You can be mindful while standing behind the cash register at work. Mindfulness can be practiced when you are in the middle of a conversation with a friend. You can even be mindful when you are on the couch alone in your house. There are many chances for someone to be mindful, and there are no set rules of when and where you can practice it. It is all up to you and the situation in which you are trying to be mindful.

There are different ways of being mindful, but as you practice more, you should come up with a method of your own. Not everyone is going to find that each of these methods works for them, so make sure you select what is most appropriate for you. These methods can be done when you are sitting on your couch and stressing over something that is out of your control. Or, if you are trying to fall asleep and the depressive thoughts won't stop, be mindful.

Furthermore, when you are at a party and you are worried about how you look or what you are saying to others, be mindful. When you see something that is triggering but you can't leave the situation, be mindful. Basically, whenever you feel like you need more than what is available to you, it is a good idea to practice Mindfulness. It can seem scary and overwhelming, but it is up to you to do your best to keep yourself grounded in reality and not in your invasive, intruding, distorted, and unhealthy thoughts.

Remember when going through these exercises that if your mind happens to drift back to anxious thoughts, don't punish yourself. Just do your best to keep redirecting your mind to the present. It will be challenging at first.

The more you practice these methods, however, the easier it will be to stay connected to the present and not drift off into the future or stay stuck in the past. You will have a better sense of how to keep thinking about the "now" rather than anything else that is causing you anxiety.

Group Mindfulness is important as well. If you work in a business setting with many other people, then you know that you can sometimes pick up on their stress, causing your own to heighten. If Mindfulness is practiced in groups, it will help everyone's health overall.

Games are a great way to be mindful. Look into free phone games you can play that will help you reduce stress. Whenever you are feeling anxious, you can play the game rather than sit with your anxious thoughts. In a group setting or in an individual sense, puzzles are also great ways to help keep you mindful. You might consider putting one on a table at a party to help keep people distracted when things aren't as active.

Look for ways that you can implement games into your daily activities. Instead of sitting around watching TV after dinner, play a game with your family to keep everyone distracted from depressive thoughts. Or, try doing word searches, sudoku, and crosswords to give you something to do with your hands. Adult coloring books are great as well.

Relaxed Detective

The following is a good exercise to center yourself and bring you to a calm state of mindfulness. Think of yourself as a detective looking for clues. Absorb the details of your surroundings. Notice color schemes of the area—the grass and the sky or the artwork and the pictures if you happen to be inside. Notice the people around you. Are they tall? Short? Notice hair colors and styles. Taking in all the details around you from the mindset of a detective can help get you centered again.

Quote Mantra

Memorize some of your favorite quotes to repeat in your head when you get stressed and need to get to a more productive, balanced state of mind. The Tao I-Ching has some good ones, for instance.

"Sixteen spokes converge on the hub of the wheel, but it is not these spokes that make the wheel useful. Rather, it is the emptiness in the middle. A potter may shape a fine vase, but it is not the vase which is important but the nothing inside which you will fill."

Quotes such as this one can help you to focus and stay centered.

Fake Yawn

Have you ever had someone yawn near you and then you find yourself yawning as well? It has happened to us all, and it can be surprisingly useful for a quick and solid dose of Mindfulness. Make a slow, fake yawn and you can induce this behavior in yourself. This gives you an instant splash of a meditative, relaxed state, and that small dose is sometimes all you need to find your focus.

Body Scan

The technique is often assisted, but it can be done alone as well. You should lie on your back, palms held at your sides. The scan begins by focusing on your breathing. Note the rhythm of your breath before focusing on the feeling in your feet, then your legs, and up along your body.

Take note of how it feels to move your toes and the feel of the exercise mat underneath you. Note any aches or pains as you slowly scan your body. Finally, when you've scanned your body in this manner and arrived at your head, finish by taking note of how your scalp feels against the pillow. Open your eyes and you will find yourself mindful and refreshed.

Seeing Mindfully

This exercise is designed to bring you to a state of mindfulness while also promoting the imagination. It can be quite serene and beautiful once you have mastered it. Find somewhere comfortable. It can be inside your house while looking out the window, or in some secluded place of nature close to you. Be sure it is secluded so that you aren't interrupted and can enjoy this exercise at its fullest. The next part is simple in explanation, but you will find implementing it may take a little practice.

Look at the world around you and let yourself absorb the details. Unlike the "Relaxed Detective," you are not going to quantify them in an empowering manner, but rather you are going to appreciate them in an aesthetic sense. If you see a dog, instead of thinking "dog," focus on the way it walks and the color of its fur. Flowers and trees become browns, greens, and yellows, and all other colors that you see across the spectrum. They become the motion that the wind imparts on them.

By taking away our names for things and focusing on their visible essence, we can achieve a meditative state of mindfulness. It is like taking our usual names for things that we see every day and putting them into a diffuser, like the light in a prism, to see the spectrum of things that make them up so that we can appreciate them in a different way. While this exercise seems almost esoteric, it has some very practical value from a logical standpoint. It relaxes you and teaches your brain to instantly assess the components of a thing so that you can appreciate and acknowledge it. "That's not a sunflower; that's a circle of orange, made of tiny orange dots with small, dark contrasts within, surrounded by brilliant yellow ovals and riding atop emerald-colored stilts." Try this one. Learning to break something down into its components will not only give you a form of instant meditation at your command but can teach you to break down complex thoughts of your own through the virtue of having practiced this technique. It is a keeper.

Listening Mindfully

This exercise is normally done in a group, but with couples who are very close and open with each other (or wish to be), it can be an immensely useful tool for obtaining a meditative state of understanding and mindfulness both with the self and with the other. It begins with sitting close together. Each person speaks, uninterrupted, about one thing that they are stressed about as well as something that they are looking forward to enjoying. When the first finishes, the other speaks about their own single stress and the thing that they are looking forward to enjoying.

The person speaking at the time should focus on their feelings about speaking and what they are saying—how their mind races or how their body feels. They should also focus on the posture of the other during their talk. The listener should focus on how they feel listening and on the speaker's body language. Thus, personal body language can be learned, which is useful enough for the whole exercise, but there is much more to be obtained from this practice.

At the close of the practice, each person describes what it was like for them both to speak and to listen. Some points to consider: How did I feel while talking? While listening? Did my mind wander at all? Did I feel judged or pass judgment?

For couples, a good closing might be for each to repeat what the other person said using their own words. No judgment should be made, but some positive affirmation can be given. Examples of closing remarks are: "Yes, that is close to/exactly what I was wanting to communicate" or "I don't feel that was everything, but we'll keep working at this so that we may both be heard."

Don't expect results overnight, but with this technique, closeness and mindfulness can be improved in the couple structure. Like anything worthwhile, a little work is involved, but you will love the results.

Life Savers

Take the first roll of candy apart and assign a particular moment of success or happiness to a color in the candy stack. Taste each flavor as you assign it as this is important to achieve the desired effect.

When you are feeling disjointed, tasked, or stressed, take a Life Saver out of your pocket, note the color, and then taste it. Think of the happy moment you've associated with it. Don't overthink it, just taste the flavor and think of your happy place, time, or moment. Savor it, enjoy the candy, and do not let yourself think of the problem until the Life Saver is finished.

Giving yourself a break to think of something positive can help you get your mind back to the logical and positive approach to life. Creating a mental reminder in the candy can help you draw upon that memory in an instant through a physical medium. Plus, the candy is portable.

Five Senses

"Five Senses" is another great technique that requires nothing but your body. For this one, don't get up and grab things, but instead, just identify them in your mind. This method takes you through all five of your senses, the ability to hear, see, touch, smell, and taste. You will also be counting down from five, so there will be less of a chance to be interrupted by more intrusive thoughts.

Start by identifying five things that you can see. These are any five things, and you just have to pick them out with your brain and your eyes. Maybe it is the couch in front of you, or the table that is holding all your stuff.

Next, find four things that you can touch. Maybe it is your own leg, or perhaps the fuzzy blanket wrapped around you. After that, pick out three things that you can hear. Perhaps the wind is knocking against the windows, or maybe there's a dog barking outside.

Now find two things that you can smell. You might not be able to smell anything easily, like a candle or perfume, but maybe the couch you are sitting on has a smell, or perhaps you live above a coffee shop.

Finally, pick out one thing that you can taste. You shouldn't actually taste this item, but there is something in the room you are in that has a flavor, so what is it? What would you be able to identify that item by? Repeat this process as often as you need to keep you grounded in the present moment.

Chapter 8 Mindfulness Training

The thing with mindfulness is that some of the most popular opinions regarding it are completely wrong. People put too much flair to it or have expectations that are absurd or unrealistic. Mindfulness is not supposed to fix you magically... for example, if you have depression, mindfulness will certainly help you become more peaceful. But you also need to take the necessary steps to deal with depression.

Here are five things that far too many people get wrong about mindfulness:

Mindfulness is not about "fixing you."

Mindfulness has never been about stopping one's thoughts

Mindfulness belongs to no religion.

Mindfulness is not meant to help you escape from reality

Mindfulness is no panacea

With all this in mind, why practice mindfulness? There are numerous reasons why you should practice mindfulness on the regular, as mentioned in the .

Mindfulness has been proven to improve lives as well as boost, among other aspects of health, and one's mental health.

Here are the top reasons why you should subscribe to the practice of mindfulness:

1: Mindfulness alleviates stress or at the very least some of it

We presently live in a "generation of stress." There is a lot of pressure on people today, and this often leads to a lot of accumulated stress. Stress will usually lead to health problems. At the very least, your mental health will suffer. Mindfulness is a great stress-prevention tool. People who practice mindfulness admit to feeling less stressed as they handle the issues that life serves them.

2: Mindfulness is more than just reducing stress levels

Certainly, stress reduction comes with mindfulness. However, the ultimate goal is not to reduce stress. The ultimate goal of mindfulness is to trigger the motion of our inner mental, emotional, and physical states. The goal is to make you more alive and more functional "in the present."

3: Mindfulness trains your body to thrive

You need to look no further than professional athletes for proof of this. Many pro athletes use mindfulness meditation to encourage peak performance. Collegiate basketball players are being coached to accept negative thoughts meditatively and transmute them into positive ones. Cycling champions have been coached to follow their breath for decades now. Big wave surfers are encouraged to brood on and transform their fears.

Sports psychologists have described these mindful techniques as being vital in the "coaching of the whole person." Once your mind is set right by mindfulness, it follows that your body will also be primed to perform at its best.

4: Mindfulness boosts creativity

Whether your art of choice is coloring, drawing writing, music, Etc., all of them have meditative practices that accompany them. The more 'present' you are, the more free your mind is and this can allow for more creative juices to flow.

5: Mindfulness strengthens your neural connections

By training your brain in mindfulness, you can build new neural pathways as well as networks in your brain, which helps you boost concentration, awareness, flexibility, and many other cognitive abilities.

6: Mindfulness reduces over-thinking and rumination

Often, what underlies anxiety is the unsavory duo of rumination and over-thinking. Once you worry about something, the brain is designed to commit to clinging onto the thing. It is very easy to be caught in a loop that has you replay every bad outcome that is possible, and this is not beneficial at all. Mindfulness helps you cease the endless worry and instead focus on the present.

7: Mindfulness boosts memory, focus, and performance

Being able to pay attention and focus on tasks at hand has to be one of the most vital cognitive abilities a human being can have. Seeing as mindfulness helps prevent mind-wandering and cluttering, it also helps you stay in the moment. You can give your undivided attention to the issues at hand. You are better able to focus on and solve problems competently.

8: Mindfulness helps greatly with emotional reactivity

Mindfulness helps you stay in the present. It makes you a "now" person. One perk that stems from this is that you are less emotionally reactive. You feel less compelled to recoil emotionally at every other thing that prods at you. You are better able to roll with the punches and only respond to those things that warrant it.

9: Mindfulness upholds cognitive flexibility

A study suggests that the practice of mindfulness not only helps you become less emotionally reactive; it also adds to your cognitive flexibility. If you observe most people that practice mindfulness (especially those who are great proponents of meditation as a tool to hone their mindfulness), you may notice that they are also great at self-observation that promptly disengages those pathways that were forged in the brain from prior incidences of learning; thus allowing incoming information to be understood in new, innovative ways.

10: Improves your general emotional health

By focusing on the present and affirming to yourself that indeed, you are valuable and effective in the present moment, you improve your self-image. You can adopt a more positive outlook on life. Two studies conducted on mindfulness meditation recorded decreased depression in more than 4,600 adults.

A study followed some 18 volunteer adults as they practiced mindfulness meditation for three years. This study unearthed that depression decreased and that these cases of reduced depression were long term in nature.

Further, cytokines, which are inflammatory chemicals that are released in response to stress may affect your mood and eventually lead to depression.

11: Reduction in Age-related memory loss

Improvements in focus and attention, as well as clarity of thought, may play a major role in keeping your mind young. And when your mind is young, your body tends to stay young as well.

Kirtan Kriya is a mindfulness meditation technique which combines a chant or mantra with repetitive finger motions in a bid to focus your thoughts. In numerous cases of age-based memory loss, this technique helped improve participants' ability to do memory retention tasks.

12: Mindfulness enables you to fight addictions better

The mental discipline and resolve that you develop through mindfulness meditation may help you deal with dependencies better. By practicing mindfulness, you are better equipped to face them head-on and break them. Your superior self-control and awareness will help you cut out addictions easier.

Research has shown that mindfulness meditation may help you learn to redirect your attention as well as boost your willpower. You will be in a better position to control your emotions as well as your impulses. Through time, you will be able to increase your understanding of the causes behind your most addictive behaviors.

One study which taught 19 recovering alcoholics meditation techniques showed that the participants who took in training and tried to apply it responded far better to their cravings compared to those that did not.

13: Mindfulness can help you handle pain better

Your perception of pain is connected to your mental state. In stressful conditions, it may be elevated.

For instance, a study used functional MRI techs in a bid to observe the activity of the brain as the participants experienced pain. Some of the participants had undergone as many as four days of mindfulness meditation training. The others had no meditation training.

The patients that had meditation training showed increased activity in the brain centers responsible for pain-control. They also reported less pain sensitivity.

With those amazing benefits you stand to benefit by practicing mindfulness, let us now learn how actually to practice mindfulness so that you know what to do to enjoy the amazing benefits this practice has to offer.

Chapter 9 Dealing with Insomnia, Anger, Fears and Phobias Thought

Insomnia, Anger, Fears, and Phobias are all common disorders that can result from a person experiencing anxiety, depression, or stress.

Insomnia

Insomnia is a sleep disorder that makes it difficult for a person to fall asleep or stay asleep and in some cases causes you to wake up early and be unable to fall back to sleep. Because of a lack of proper sleep, a person usually feels tired after waking up. Insomnia disorder is bad because it saps out your energy, affects your mood and health as well as your performance at work.

Enough sleep varies from one individual to the next, but the recommended sleep for adults is seven to eight hours of sleep each night. At a certain point in most adult's lives, a person may experience acute insomnia that can last for several days or weeks. However, there are people that suffer from prolonged periods of chronic insomnia. This type of insomnia may be associated with other conditions that need medical attention.

With simple daily habits, one can overcome insomnia and go back to enjoying healthy sleep patterns. How does a person know they are suffering from insomnia? Insomnia has various distinct symptoms. These may include:

- Finding it difficult to fall asleep during bedtime

- Losing sleep in the halfway through the night

- Getting up very early

- Feeling tired even after a night's sleep

- Feeling tired during the day and sleepy

- Being irritable, anxious and depressed

- Finding it hard to be attentive, focused on assignments or remembering

- Having a higher rate of mistakes and accidents

- Being constantly worried about sleep.

When should one see a doctor?

If the lack of sleep is so severe that you find it hard to function in your day to day activities, seeing a doctor is advisable. The doctor should work with you to identify the cause of insomnia and come up with various treatment options. In case the doctor feels that you are suffering from a sleep disorder, he may recommend you see a sleep specialist.

How age relates to insomnia

Insomnia can be directly related to one's age. The older a person gets, the more they experience insomnia. When a person gets older, they experience:

- Your sleep pattern changes – as a person ages, sleep becomes less. Slight noise or other changes in one's environment can cause a person to wake up frequently. Age causes the internal clock to advance, making one tired earlier at night and waking up even earlier. Regardless, it is healthy to have the same amount of sleep when older just like a younger person.

- Changes in what you do – if you are less active during the day may cause you to take an afternoon nap. This, in the end, will interfere with your sleep at night.

- Change in health – if a person experiences chronic pain from conditions like arthritis or back pains, they may have challenges sleeping. Other conditions like anxiety or depression, also interfere with sleep. Other medical issues may cause frequent urinating at night, such as bladder problems, diabetes among others. Restless leg syndrome and sleep apnea are also other conditions that interrupt sleep patterns.

- Prescription drugs – older people use more prescription medicines than younger people do. This increases the chance of developing chronic insomnia.

Insomnia can also affect children and teenagers, as well. However, most of the causes at this age is due to their irregular patterns in their sleep schedules. Lack of sleep can also be associated with some risks in specific individuals.

The risk of suffering from insomnia is greater if:

- The individual is a woman. Shifts in the hormones during the menstrual cycle or menopause play a significant role. When a woman is going through menopause, they experience hot flashes as well as night sweats that will interrupt sleep. Pregnant mothers also experience insomnia due to hormonal changes.

- If you are over the age of 60, then your chances of suffering from insomnia are high. As you age, you experience changes in health increasing the risk of insomnia.

- If you are experiencing a mental health disorder or a physical health condition, you are at a greater risk of developing insomnia.

- Stress is another condition that increases insomnia. When a person is undergoing stressful situations, they may suffer from temporary insomnia. However, prolonged periods of stress may also result in chronic insomnia in many individuals.

- Lack of regular schedule is another contributor to insomnia. A person that often travels across different time zones or works with various shifts is likely to experience insomnia.

Insomnia Complications

Just like having a healthy diet is important, having healthy sleep patterns is also important, as well as regular physical exercise. Regardless of the reasons causing your lack of sleep, insomnia can physically and mentally affect you negatively. Individuals with insomnia have a lower quality of life as compared to individuals that enjoy good sleeping habits.

Various complications associated with insomnia include:

- Poor performance at work or school
- Decreased reaction time on the road that may result in higher risks of accidents
- Mental health disorders like anxiety, substance abuse, and depression
- Higher risk of long-term diseases such as heart diseases.

Practical strategies that will help you sleep better.

Developing good sleep habits can help prevent insomnia and cause a person to enjoy a sound sleep. Some practical things you can do to improve your sleep will include:

- Be consistent in your bed and wake time even during the weekends.

- Be active. Regular physical activity will aid in promoting good night sleep

- Check your medications if one of the side effects is lack of sleep. If so, speak to your doctor to switch the medicine

- Try and avoid day time naps, and if you feel you must, limit the duration.

- Limit or avoid entirely the use of nicotine, alcohol or caffeine

- Avoid taking huge meals before bedtime and taking of sugary beverages

- Don't use your bedroom as a work station or a place for entertainment. Use it only for the intended purpose.

- Come up with a bedtime ritual that is relaxing, like taking a warm shower, listening to soft music in low volume, or reading.

Anger

Anger is a state of emotion that varies from mild irritation to full-blown rage of fury. Anger, just like other emotions is accompanied by biological and physical changes. When a person gets angry, their heart rate and blood pressure shoot up. The energy and hormonal levels also increase with anger.

A person can experience anger from internal or external stimulants. You can be angry because of a certain person or event, or from being worried and brooding on your personal issues. Having traumatic memories of events that were enraging can also cause anger feelings.

How do people express anger?

Naturally, a human being expresses anger by responding aggressively. Anger is a natural way to respond to threats. It results in aggressive feelings and behaviors that allow you to be defensive to protect yourself when attacked. For one's survival, a certain amount of anger is acceptable.

On the extreme, a person can lash out physically at any person or thing that annoys and irritates him. Social norms and law work to limit how far a person can express their angry feelings.

A person uses a variety of processes to deal with anger. These processes can be unconscious or conscious. There are three approaches to dealing with anger, through expressing your anger feelings, suppressing them, and finding calm. Depending on an individual, you can deal with anger by:

- Expressing your anger. A person should express their feelings of anger, not in an aggressive way but assertively. In order to do this, a person needs to learn how to clearly express their needs and formulate ways to get them met without hurting other people. When a person is assertive, it does not mean they are demanding or pushy; it is respectful of you as well as of others.

- Suppressing your anger. You can decide to suppress, convert, or redirect your anger. This is usually when a person holds their anger in, stops thinking about the situation, and focuses on something positive. This technique is aimed at inhibiting your anger feelings and converting those feelings to more constructive things or behavior. However, this approach can be dangerous. With no outward expression of anger, it can turn inward and can cause depression, high blood pressure or hypertension.

Anger that has not been expressed can cause many problems. It can result in pathological expressions such as passive-aggressive behavior. This is where a person decides to get back at people indirectly without their knowledge instead of directly confronting them. A person that suppresses anger can also develop a cynical and hostile personality. This is a person that will always put others down, criticize, and make cynical comments. A person with these strains most often fails in having healthy and successful relationships.

- Calming down inside is another way of dealing with anger. This involves taking control of your outward behavior as a result of the anger feelings as well as your internal responses. You can do this by finding a way to lower your heart rate, calming yourself, and allowing the feelings to subside.

Fears and Phobias

Phobias and fears are types of anxiety disorders. A fear develops into a phobia when a person is expected to change their lifestyle to manage it. A phobia can be defined as an extreme or irrational dread or fear that is aroused by a particular situation or object to the extent that it affects your life.

If a person is suffering from a phobia, they will go to great lengths to stay away from a situation or an object that other people may be considering it to be harmless. The good news is that you do not need to live with phobias because they are treatable conditions. It is possible to overcome a phobia. Some phobias are easier for a person to live with because they do not affect their daily life. For instance, the fear of snakes, also called ophiophobia, will not affect your day-to-day life. On the other hand, agoraphobia, which is fear of open spaces, can make it difficult for a person to lead a normal life.

If a phobia starts to interfere with your daily life, it is time to seek help. In some severe cases, a person may have to stop working because they are unable to take public transport. This kind of phobia can interfere with a person's way of life, and statistics show that it affects about 8% of the UK population.

Fears and phobias can be specific. They may include fear of heights, spiders or dentists, or generalized kind of phobias or fears.

Some of the common phobias include:

- Social phobia – this is the fear of social interactions.

- Agoraphobia – This is when a person is afraid of open public spaces

- Emetophobia – this is when a person is afraid of vomiting

- Erythrophobia – this is the fear of blushing

- Driving phobia – as the name suggests, it is the fear to drive

- Hydrochodria – this is the fear of getting sick

- Aerophobia – this is the fear of flying

- Arachnophobia – this is the fear of spiders

- Zoophobia – the fear of animals

- Claustrophobia – the fear of spaces that are confined.

A person that suffers from a social phobia may have started by being just shy. When this behavior is exaggerated to the point that it disrupts a person's life, it is time to seek treatment.

How do phobias start?

No one knows exactly how phobias develop. However, certain phobias are believed to originate from childhood, mostly between the age of 4 and 8.

Agoraphobia and social phobia often start later in life. These phobias start mostly at puberty or in the later teenage years and earlier twenties. According to psychologists, a good way to eliminate some fears in children is by familiarizing them with the objects of their fear.

Treating Phobias

Some certain phobias may require exposure to the item that generates fear in a person. Treatment can also be through a form of self-exposure therapy. This is a form of Cognitive Behavioral Therapy where the victim can use self-help books or join support groups to deal with the phobias.

Exposure therapy – this focuses on changing the response of the victim to the situation or object that causes fear. This is done gradually but repeatedly exposing oneself to the source of the specific phobia. With constant exposure, the thoughts and feelings you experience will cause you to start managing them. Start managing your anxious feelings about the situation by imagining yourself in it and then gradually exposing yourself to the situation.

Cognitive-behavioral therapy (CBT) – this involves using exposure while combining with other techniques. A person is told to learn various ways to cope and view with the object of their fear. You develop different beliefs about your phobias and body sensations, as well as the impact they have on your daily life. CBT focuses on helping a person learn to master or control their thoughts and feelings instead of feeling overwhelmed by them.

Chapter 10 Progressive Muscle Relaxation

We hold tension in our muscles and connective tissues when we are stressed. By intentionally tensing and then relaxing our muscles we trigger a reduction in our mental tension as well.

1. Sit comfortably in a peaceful room, or lay in bed if you plan on sleeping afterwards.
2. Take a few deep breaths and relax your body. I prefer to close my eyes, but that is up to you.
3. Tense all the muscles of your left foot and hold for 5 seconds.
4. Relax your foot for 5 seconds and imagine it sinking down.
5. Notice the change in sensation as the tension is released.
6. Repeat steps 3 through 5 for each muscle group on each side of your body, progressing upwards towards your head: lower leg, upper leg, buttocks, stomach, chest & back, fingers, hands, lower arms, upper arms, shoulders, neck, face, and forehead.

Variations:

1. If you are up for a challenge you can also try the imaginary version of this. Follow the same progression from foot to head, but this time only imagine what it would be like to tense and release without actually moving the muscles. I find this can put you in an even more relaxed mental state, especially by the time your reach your temple.

2. Another variation is to imagine your body as a hollow vessel slowly filling up with a rejuvenating energy that glows with intensity on every in-breath. Imagine a churning golden vapour working its way up from your feet to your head. Feel the intensity growing with each breath and culminating in the middle of your forehead or "third eye" point.

3. A fast and easy variant is to rest your hands on your legs, palms down, and imagine a flow of energy surging from the base of each finger towards the tip, one at a time in a continuous

cycle. I do this one regularly because it takes very little effort to get results.

Tips:

1. Hold your muscles tight but not to the point of pain.
2. The whole process should only take 10-20 minutes, but if you are short on time, or just not in the mood for complexity, simply hold all the muscles of your body tight at once for 10 seconds then release.
3. You can find YouTube videos and phone apps to help guide you if you'd rather not think at all. You may like to consider listening to a guided self-hypnosis recording as well.

Chapter 11 Transforming Anxiety into Your Driving Force

We feel anxious around various people, things, or even animals. Due to this, our confidence is compromised in a bid to create a balance of emotions in the body. Anxiety and self-confidence are directly related in the sense that an increase in anxiety will lead to a decrease in the other variable and vice versa. Poor self-confidence does not always end up as a success story. When anxiety first dawns on you, accept it learn it, and embrace it in order to prevent it from taking advantage of you again. The lack of self-confidence can be pegged on a number of factors that are not limited to the phobia of being assessed by others. This is often as a result of always looking at yourself in the shoes of others. In order to overcome this condition, one needs to take himself outside the context of a group and visualize themselves as individuals.

Staying conscious and knowing your fears is one way of overcoming this kind of feeling. As long as we are wary of the situations that keep our feet on toes, we can learn to embrace them and in turn, we live a better life that is not full of self-criticism. When self-confidence overpowers anxiety, we tend to be obliged to think on the positive mostly and as a result, anxiety levels drop.

There are a number of practices that might be of key importance when dealing with stress levels.

Know that you have a controlling effect of about forty percent on what you experience.

As human beings, what we experience has a lot of impact in our thinking which in turn affects what we do thus our actions. What we experience either influences us negatively or positively according to how we process our information. In a bid to secure happiness, we are influenced by goals that we set to achieve and the relationships that we are in either consanguinity or affinity.

Your focus should be on events that have a positive effect

When something positive happens, you should take time and acknowledge yourself for that. This has an effect on building self-confidence. It, in turn, helps store the events in the long-term memory.

Fake it until you feel it. You are obviously feeling anxious because your self-confidence has left you deserted and suddenly you feel like you are all alone. This feeling can be eradicated by bringing in face value of what you want to feel. Keep the face value until it becomes part of you. This will involve doing a reality check on yourself and changing a few things on how you operate. For instance, that embraces a posture that is apt, smile, pretend to feel at home.

Moreover, there are a number of ways in which an individual with anxiety disorders may channel the anxiety into a driving force. The issue with people with anxiety disorders is not the feeling itself but rather the response towards the overwhelming adrenaline. There are a number of responses that may be of aid:

Channel the adrenaline

When one is anxious, the adrenal glands secrete a hormone that is known as adrenaline. Adrenaline is often enhanced by other products such as caffeine. When the body is producing adrenaline, this means that its functioning is at its optimum and that you are able to engage in a number of activities at the same time. Instead of holding back to this kind of energy, one needs to convert it into a helping agent rather than sitting on it.

When it comes to sports, being anxious is the best way to enter a game. Anxiety keeps the players hyped and focused. With all the overwhelming emotions, particularly phobia, research has it that there is some amount of sweetness that comes with one being anxious. Further, the brain processed a lot of information at ago when the anxiety levels are slightly heightened. Adrenaline has its pros and cons. The only way of living through anxiety is by using the pros to your advantage.

Re-assess your anxiety

Most people have a pre-determined tendency that is directed towards anxiety. People always associate anxiety with negative events that happen in their lives. They tend to believe that when they are feeling anxious, a bad deed usually tends to ensue. This may not be the case. The difference between a feeling of excitement and a feeling of nervousness is almost the same and can be replaced with one for the other. People tend to confuse this fact, and that is why they always relate anxiety to bad deeds. Naturally, our bodies are meant to respond to stressful events through being anxious. When an individual is excited, the focus is often directed to success rather than failures.

Anticipate the subtlety of anxiety

When engaging various tasks, an individual may feel anxious or excited depending on the past experiences of that particular individual. The best way to overcome such feelings is being in a position to understand and accept anxiety as part of you. Most individuals will be inclined to the thought that artificial counter-measures may be of aid. This may not be the case since they only operate on a short term basis. The more comfortable you will be around anxiety is the only way that you will learn to live with it.

Transforming anxiety into motivation

In order to transform your anxiety into motivation, you need to find the urge behind looking for a motivating factor. With a little anxiety, just enough to keep an individual on course, this is the urge that you need to find. Whatever the worry maybe, this urge will often act against its forces. You will be thinking of a solution to your problem even before you know it. Anxiety often happens in anticipation of the occurrence of a future event that is directly or indirectly related to you. The right levels of anxiety keep you proper, but when the levels sky-rocket, the demerits fall squarely on you.

Differentiate between productive tension and non-productive tension

Productive tension entails focusing on the events that can be influenced by you. This includes focusing on how to better yourself and move forward. Unproductive tension, on the other hand, adopts a form of wishful thinking since the thoughts of an individual are glued on events that he or she has no control over whatsoever.

For instance, if your tension is focused on a game that you are supposed to play, you will acknowledge your fears and take the requisite steps for instance training in order to make sure that you are up to the task when it falls in your coat. Unproductive thinking, for instance, is when you worry about the feelings of another person. This you have no control over totally.

Make your anxiety devoid of adversity

The anticipated outcome should not take the better part of you to the extent that you see the worst-case scenarios. Do the math in your head. Evaluate the probabilities. In light of this, be honest to yourself. When you have a calculated risk in mind, you tend to know its severity, and in turn, your anxiety levels will drop.

The art of centering

Centering entails a practice that enables you to do to carry out a performance strategy prior to the actual one. Centering acts as a method of calming down the mind and making it focus on a particular aim. In order for one to achieve centering, there are a number of steps that need to be followed:

An individual needs to select his or her point of concentration. This is often referred to as the focal point. After this has been done, one needs to establish a candid goal. There is usually a desire to achieve that has been covered up by the anxious mind. An individual needs to have an already established mindset about where they wish to go and what they wish to achieve. This should be stated in a positive language in order to trigger a positive response. When breathing, make sure that you take various episodes of breathing in and out since this helps to calm your nerves. Tension is what eats up most individuals. Know your pressure points and when to release them. This will help you to relax more. When the body is tensed, you may not be able to achieve optimum functioning.

A person's energy rests specifically at the center of the body. Finding this entre is what will act as your driving force throughout your anxiety expedition. In order to succeed in the goals that you have set, you need to see yourself succeeding. Have the right mindset, one that is embraced by a winner. This will push you towards the desired results. The energy flowing through your body needs to be appropriately channeled. In this feeling of calm, you can now be fully in control of your energy. One should be careful enough to know when to see a therapist. This is because there are some levels of anxiety that are not advisable.

Chapter 12 Breaking Free From Anxiety

The process of overcoming anxiety can be hard to wrap one's head around; however, looking at the cycle of anxiety can be at least a little easier to understand once the seasons are brought into the mix. As the seasons change so does the emotional and physical feelings a person feels along the way. When the weather gets cold and the sun does not seem to be as warming, it is not uncommon for a person's mood to also take a dip. People are not as interested in braving the cold weather so more time may be spent inside.

The downside to this is that fresh air has been linked to being able to lift a person's mood after they were to feel down. There are even some disorders that are in direct correlation to the winter weather like seasonal affective disorder.

Once the weather begins to warm and people are more inclined to go outside, they are also more likely to become more active than they had been during the colder months. This is effective for a person's mental health because, similar to getting fresh air, exercise has been linked to lifting a person's spirits as well as their mood.

Along with the shift in weather patterns, there may also be times that a person gets excited by the changes that come along with it. People can become excited about being able to see their friends in the summer months or an upcoming vacation. Maybe someone has a favorite holiday that gets them looking forward to a particular season. However, there are also events and thoughts that can lead to a person becoming anxious over what is to come. The person may be aware that they are facing challenges in the upcoming months, may that be at work or with a family member.

With all of the different changes a person may experience in their life, this may be a cause as to why anxiety disorders are some of the most prevalent mental disorders in the American culture. Unfortunately, the understanding of what anxiety is not as widely known as it should be. This is partly due to the fact that people oftentimes mistake their anxiety for being moments of stress; however, the two are completely different.

The best way to better understand the difference between the pair is to take a deeper look into what both stress and anxiety entail. Stress is generally considered to be the reaction to an external cause. An external cause could be a looming deadline a person is trying to meet at work or an argument between two friends.

Also, when a person is experiencing stress, their feelings of negative intensity will usually diminish once the experience has ended. This is because stress is a person's thought, attitude, or feeling as though they do not have the necessary internal assets to meet the external demands. Once the event is over, then they no longer have to be concerned about the issue.

Anxiety, on the other hand, is a person's individual reaction to their stress. Unlike stress, anxiety originates in a person's internal experience, specifically through their thoughts and emotions. Also, while stress comes out when a person is in the mists of an impending stressful situation or the situation is currently happening, anxiety can oftentimes originate even during a moment that would not typically develop in people. Furthermore, those feelings of anxiety continue to persist even after the event has ended. The anxiety may not be at its most extreme but it still lingers in the background of a person's mind.

An example of how anxiety might linger in a person's thoughts is if two friends have a fight. Maybe one of the friends said some hurtful things and even though the pair ended up making up, the friend who said the hurtful words might still feel guilty about what they said even though their friend forgave them.

By keeping the above example in mind, it makes it easier to see why anxiety is oftentimes connected to rumination, which is when a person goes over and over the same exact problem or thought without coming to a conclusion. The longer a person mulls over those same thoughts continuously, the harder it becomes to move on from their negative thoughts. As a result, this makes it more difficult for someone to overcome those negative thoughts.

Another major issue that comes out when a person is experiencing anxiety is described as an anxiety overload. This is when a person's external burdens crash into their usual reactions. An instance where this could happen is if a person is about to walk into an important meeting at their job. In situations such as the above example, the person's body seems to disappear once their mind becomes overly consumed with all of the worries, suspicions, and the overall range of mental states the person may have to flood their mind.

***

Even though anxiety and stress are two completely different issues that go on within a person's mind, the ways in which a person can try and push past each of them can be the same for both. When a person is ready to stop the negative consequences of their stress and anxiety, they can look into a few tips that will do wonders on their mental state in the moment and in the long-run.

The first tip is to keep reminding one's self that their anxiety and stress may occur in the present moment, but the negative feelings will pass. An example would be, a mom is on maternity leave. Thanksgiving is right around the corner, and she is hosting the family gathering this year. She is trying to make sure the how is in order and she has all of the ingredients she needs for what she is cooking for the feast. However, one of her kids is home sick with a fever and the other is only a little over a year old. She is cleaning the bathroom when one kid is calling for her to bring them some crackers while the other kid is crying because they have woken up from their nap.

Everyone has some type of experience where they feel as though they have multiple responsibilities or issues pilling upon them and they do not have enough time and energy to get it all done. That is a trademark of stress, which can lead to anxiety if the person's worries and fears of not getting the tasks done become all-encompassing.

The best way to overcome those negative feelings is for a person to recognize that the feelings that they are having are actually an extremely common emotional state that is usually considered to be anxiety. Even though the feelings are likely uncomfortable, the negative feelings will eventually go away. It is actually when a person attempts to fight their feelings of anxiety that ends up making the anxiety even worse. It is important that people remember this, and to also keep in mind that when a person is able to accept the negative feelings anxiety evokes, that will lead to the natural relaxation response the human body has.

The second tip people should consider looking into centers around the idea of self-soothing. Every single person will experience moments in their life where they are forced to face-off against an anxiety-ridden situation. When a person is put into a situation like one where a boss is hunting down an employee for a report that has not yet been finished, the employee's sympathetic nervous system spontaneously triggers physiological changes to their body. During this process, a person will find their breath quickens, their heartbeat begins to race, and adrenaline is secreted. All of those natural responses of the body are a person's survival mechanisms, which is also known as their fight-or-flight response. The intended goal of this response is to help a person get away from a real-life emergency or danger they are currently facing.

However, when anxiety and stress occur but do not pose any imminent danger in a person, the fight-or-flight response that still rises in not necessary. This is when the person should be implementing self-soothing techniques to stop the fight-or-flight response created from an imaginary "threat." There are three particular techniques that have been known to be extremely effective with soothing a person.

The first technique focuses on the practice of Diaphragmatic Breathing. This is when a person uses breathing techniques to trigger a relaxation response that results in a person's heart rate decreasing back to a normal pace. People are not able to deliberately change their pulse, which means other concrete options must be used instead. That is why breathing techniques are quite effective when it comes to lowering a person's heart rate.

One particular breathing technique that is used more often than any other breathing technique is one in which a person contracts their diaphragm. The diaphragm is the horizontal muscle in the chest which is located directly above the stomach cavity. People may also know this same exercise by the names of belly breathing or abdominal breathing, which all serve the same purpose.

The second type of self-soothing technique is when a person talks positively to themselves. More often than not people speak to children in a way that promotes compassion. This is partly due to the fact that most people know better than to treat a child with anything other than kindness, but also because it is common for people to instinctively try to help other people when they are stressed. That being said, most people do a much better job of helping other people who are stressed than they do with helping themselves when they have stress and anxiety in their life.

In order for a person to be able to increase their personal emotional comfort, it is vital that the person takes the time to practice both realistic self-talk and how to reassure one's self. By keeping that in mind, the next time a person finds that they are feeling anxious, they should try out a variety of phrases such as, "I know that I can get through this" or "I am aware of my current anxiety, but I know that I hold the power to calm myself down."

One other type of self-soothing technique is to try out muscle relaxation. One of the most common components of stress is for a person's muscles to tense and tighten. The main goal of the muscle relaxation exercise is to increase a person's relaxed state as well as their physical comfort. The process of tightening up and releasing the muscle tension begins with a person's largest muscle group, the glutes.

The third tip for reducing anxiety and stress is to look at the person's diet and see if any changes should be made in it. What people choose to eat and drink plays a major role in their emotional state. Any foods that contain caffeine or alcohol are thought to heavily amplify an individual's anxiety levels. Even when alcohol or caffeine are consumed in small doses, there have still been studies that have found the anxiety levels I a person will rise.

The danger of consuming too much caffeine and alcohol can have actual damaging effects on a person's health, one of the issues being panic attacks. Caffeine has also been known to lead to some physical symptoms such as shaking and trembling.

Even though the negative effects of caffeine are very much real, the act of cutting the substance out abruptly can lead to a person developing withdrawal symptoms because of the product's addictive quality. Some of those withdrawal symptoms like headaches, irritability, and restlessness are also common symptoms of stress and anxiety. It is for that reason that withdrawing from caffeine too hastily can also heighten a person's anxiety symptoms. That is one of the reasons why it is so important that a person gradually takes caffeine out of their diet rather than all at once.

Similar to caffeine, alcohol is usually consumed when a person wants to "take the edge off" or during social interactions. However, one of the main drawbacks of alcohol is that it dehydrates the human body which typically leads to higher levels of stress in an individual.

The combination of alcohol and dehydration in the body leads to an imbalance of bacteria in a person's gut, which will also lead to anxiety symptoms rising to the surface. A research study conducted at McMaster University found that a person's bacterial balance in their body affects their mood more so than any other possible factors.

The next possible way a person could reduce their stress and anxiety is by taking the time to get up and move. It is no secret that exercise is a necessary component of maintaining a person's health; however, people may not be aware of all of the possible benefits of exercise, including the positive effect exercise can have on a person's mental health.

Research that has been conducted over the past few decades has looked into the possibility that exercise can be more effective for an individual's mental state than medicine might. This may be due to the fact that a regular exercise routine can ease a person's stress as well as improve their mood, self-esteem, and overall energy levels.

When a person is exercising, their body is releasing the neurotransmitter known on endorphins. During this process, the endorphins connect with receptors in the brain, which leads to feelings of happiness. The process also is known for being able to help with any physical pain a person may be having.

One other possible tip a person could attempt to utilize for anxiety and stress reduction is to make sure the person is getting enough sleep. When a person has a bad night's sleep, it does not come as a shock that a person would become cranky. Unfortunately, restlessness and disturbances in sleep can be extremely common in numerous emotional disorders, especially the types of anxiety ones. The result of restless sleep for those who have a mental disorder is that their symptoms tend to worsen. Although, it can be difficult to pinpoint whether a person's stress and anxiety come before a disruption in their sleep pattern or if it happens the other way around.

Multiple studies have been conducted to get a better understanding of the effects a lack of sleep can have on the mind, body, and spirit. One credible find is that even when a person only loses a couple of hours of sleep, their feelings of stress, exhaustion, sadness, and anger will increase. The good news is that a person can look into different tips that will help them to regulate their sleep cycle. A few of the noteworthy tips include going to bed and waking up at the same time every day, eating dinner at the same time each night, and getting out of bed if a person wakes up in the middle of the night and struggles to fall back to sleep.

Chapter 13 Learn to Get Better

Trying cognitive behavioral therapy or other treatments for the first time can be daunting, especially if you feel you've tried everything and nothing has worked. Unraveling anxiety might feel like you're exposing yourself to more pain. However, the outcome is worth it. Below is a list of ways that overcoming anxiety will change your life.

- Your life goals will be easier to achieve. When you are no longer fearful and avoiding situations, you will feel free to pursue that promotion or take that once-in-a-lifetime trip. Goals that seemed out of reach will suddenly become realistic.

- You will think more positively about your future. Anxiety tends to cast a negative outlook on what is yet to come. When you are free of anxiety, you will feel more hopeful about what is around the next corner.

- It will be easier to cope with medical conditions. You won't worry unnecessarily about your physical health, but rather will do what is necessary to take care of yourself. Visits to the doctor will no longer fill you with anxiety and dread.

- You may feel relief from depression or low mood. When anxiety is relieved, depression and low mood often show improvement as well. Along with feeling less anxious, you may feel more optimistic, have more energy, sleep better, and generally have more interest in life.

- Anxiety will no longer define you as a person. If you have long-held beliefs about yourself that center around being anxious, those will be replaced with feelings of self-esteem and self-worth. You will get to know the person you can be without those anxious thoughts.

- You will take better care of yourself. Overcoming anxiety will shed light on areas of your life that have been neglected. You will give more importance to things like nutrition, exercise, and being present in the moment.

- Relationships and work that have suffered will improve. You might develop new social connections or feel less dependent on people you have leaned on in the past. Your increased ability to concentrate will make work seem like less of a chore, and you might even find yourself seeking advancement in the workplace.

• You will feel increased enjoyment in life and more confidence. Anxiety has a way of zapping your confidence and happiness. If you've felt like every day you were just "getting through," you will now start each day confidently and in search of joy.

Chapter 14 Rediscovering the Joy of Life

At the end of the day, the main aim of trying to change the mind is to help you live a happy life. If you are already living a happy life and you are contented with your success, there is no need to go through the process of rewiring your brain. However, if you feel that you are falling short in your achievements and life goals, you need to try changing your mentality. Now that you know all the factors that affect your brain and how they link to your longer memory, we have to look at the solutions. How do you get rid of all the negative voices and start focusing on the positives? Is there hope for people who have been abused, suffered traumatic instances, and those who have lost trust in life? The simple answer is yes, there is hope for everyone. Every person has the ability to change their lives by changing their minds. You can choose to change your perspective of life and remove any limitations from your brain. You can decide to think outside the box and live a life that is full of happiness. You can choose to love and be loved without fears or worries of this world. However, this will only happen after a total mind shift. If you have been feeding your mind the negative experiences of this world, you must be willing to let them out. You must be willing to let go of your beliefs, perceptions, and superstitions. This process of brain rewiring is supposed to help you resent your brain to factory mode. In other words, we are going to take away any attachment to memories from the past. Although you may not forget some events and the data that has been packaged in your brain, you can change the information on that data. If you have a memory that causes you to fear, you can decide to turn it to confidence.

The process of mind rewiring should take about 3 to 6 weeks, depending on your practices. We have already talked about the need to change your friends to positive ones. We have talked about getting rid of habits and creating routines. You can only change your thinking by changing your actions. We have mentioned the need to think positively and to sharpen your emotional intelligence.

How to Build Positive Thoughts

Mindfulness is a type of meditation that is self-centered. In this type of meditation, a person focuses their thoughts and senses on themselves. When you practice mindfulness, you are aware of your personality, your body, your internal and external organs, your thoughts, and your feelings. For some people, mindfulness is very scary at the beginning. Most people never think about themselves. If you have never thought about yourself and the things you like, you need to start practicing mindfulness.

Mindfulness is a technique that sharpens self-awareness. When you are self-aware, you can describe what you love. You may describe yourself in all dimensions, including the way you feel about your body. This process reveals a lot of information about yourself that may not be pleasing

However, if you want to rewire your brain, you have to go through this process. One of the important principles of mindfulness is that it's a non-judgmental process. In other words, you do not judge yourself for having a certain stand on life. You do not excuse yourself for loving certain aspects of your body and hating others. Mindfulness puts you in a free space of your originality. In this free space, you can talk dirty to yourself. You can see the dirty desires in your mind and indulge in every aspect of your personality that you are afraid of revealing to the world.

During the early stages, you do not have to practice mindfulness for long. You can just practice the meditation for about 15 minutes each day. However, as you advance, you will start making deeply hidden discoveries about yourself and your personality.

The desires you have about yourself will help you determine the extent to which life experiences have messed up your thinking process. A clear observation of your desires, ambitions, and goals will help you know whether you are positive or negative. Once you start realizing the side of life you subscribe to, you are in a position to implement change. Changing the mind is not a simple process that will happen overnight. You must take time and observe your emotions and determine whether they are negative or positive. Once you can label your thoughts either positive or negative, you have to start releasing the negative ones out

Mindful meditation is designed to help you without judging. Some of the characteristics of mindfulness meditation include:

Self Control: Unlike other forms of meditation, it is self-centered. It only includes focusing on one's body and feeling. With other forms of meditation, you may focus on giving out to the world. With mindfulness, you selfishly look at yourself, your thoughts, and your opinions. Mindfulness takes away the negativity associated with a person's life by society.

No judgment: Mindfulness encourages practitioners to look at themselves without judgment. Think of the world as a place without laws. If there were no laws or societal expectations, everything you do would be deemed right. Mindful meditation encourages us to think in a way that does not put labels on behavior or character. In this type of thinking, you open your mind up to the things that you love. You may love something but fear to pursue it due to life circumstances or due to laws. However, when you practice mindfulness, you take yourself to a free space where you will not be judged for what you do.

No limits: Because the human mind has got no limits, practicing mindfulness is the perfect opportunity for you to live your dreams. In your mindful meditation, you think about the desires that are deeply ingrained in your subconscious mind. You do not worry about the things that people have to say, but rather, you focus on the things that your body and mind want. There is no limit to your desires, and there should be no limit to your feelings or dreams. Your desires can go as wild as possible. This is a free space where no one can ever take away your freedom of thought.

Self embracing: It is advisable to avoid trying mindful meditation if you are not ready to embrace your strengths and weaknesses. This type of meditation calls for self-love and self-acceptance. During mindful meditation, you may realize that you have a bigger body than you thought. You may realize that some parts of your body are not as appealing as you desired. You may also realize that your personal feelings, thoughts, and desires are not beautiful. However, for you to benefit from mindful meditation, you must maintain self-love. No matter how bad your brain may seem, you should still love yourself. You should still choose to love yourself and pride in your personality.

Awareness to change: If you are going to benefit from mindful practices, you should be able to record your feelings and also perceive change as it happens. Over a while, as you practice mindfulness, you may try implementing some behavior change practices. You shod be in a position to perceive change when it happens. Change may happen after a long time of mindful meditation. When it does happen, you should be in a position to perceive it.

Non-Biased: If you are a person who tends to be biased when making decisions, you need to change your mentality during mindful meditation. Mindful meditations are aimed at helping you achieve success in life. For this reason, the results you get from your meditation must be 100 percent accurate. If you try changing the results, you may not be helped. Just keep your mind flow without influencing it. In the beginning, this practice may be difficult. It takes some time to concentrate on one part of the body. However, as you get used to it, you will become an expert. An expert in mindful meditation can be drowned in their world for more than 3 hours. When you meditate in a mindfulness design, you are taken to a safe space where you feel peace and calm. The process of meditation itself helps you get rid of negativity. However, the process is also vital in observing negativity and creating solutions.

Participatory observation: This is the hardest aspect of mindfulness. it may seem as if mindfulness is a passive observation of the occurrences in your body. On the contrary, a mindfulness practitioner is a participant in the process. When it comes to thoughts and feelings, you must let them flow naturally while at the same time, you observe them. In some instances, there is a risk if trying to influence your thoughts. However, if you get used to it, you start learning how to differentiate your thoughts from the observations. The thoughts are part of your body, yet you also have to observe them one by one.

Practice Peace, Love and Kindness Meditation

We have already talked about peace, love, and kindness meditation. This is one of the options you have if you want to live a happy life and deal with all the negative thoughts in your mind. Just to help you practice this type of meditation, here is a simple step by step guide.

Step 1: Prepare the meditation room

Just like all other types of meditation, this type of meditation requires a quiet place with minimal interactions. You should have a clear timeframe for your meditation in mind when preparing the room. For instance, if you will be meditating for about 1 hour, you must ensure that the room will remain uninterrupted for an hour from the time of start. Any person interrupting your session may force you to start all over. Your meditation room will need a few essentials, such as a meditation mat or chair and music, if possible. However, it is not necessary to have music. You can still practice your meditation in a quiet environment.

Step 2: Setting Yourself Up for Meditation

Once you have your room and all the necessary essentials in place, you should be ready to start your sessions. First, you need to find the right sitting posture. For the meditation session to be successful, you must prepare your muscles well. Do a bit of stretching before positioning yourself. You should note that sometimes muscles get tired during meditation. Muscle straining is not good, especially during meditation. You do not want muscle cramps disrupting your session when you are busy trying to enjoy your meditation session.

To practice meditation, you should position yourself on the mat while sitting in an upright posture. Cross your legs in front and allow your hands to fall on your thighs freely. If you are using a chair, it must be a right-backed chair. Sit in your chair with your back positioned parallel to the back of the chair. In this manner, you will be sitting in an upright position. To ensure that you are positioned well, try breathing a large chunk of air. The sitting position should allow your lungs to take in plenty of air without straining. Once you feel that you are comfortable and that you can breathe well, move on to the next step.

Step 3: Prepare your mind for meditation

Before you get into peace, love, and kindness meditation, you have to bring your senses together. Any person who suffers from anxiety, depression, and other mental disorders is likely to have many thoughts flowing in the head. However, this is the time to get rid of such thoughts. Before you start your meditation, just close your eyes and focus on the darkness. Try as much as possible to focus your mind on the darkness. This exercise should help you bring your thoughts together and move away from your negative thoughts. If you are afraid of darkness, you may also just open your eyes and choose an item in the room to focus on. Just pick any item in the room; it could be a picture on the wall, it can be a seat or a pencil. Any item in front of you can be used to focus your thoughts. When focusing on that item, try to describe it in your mind. Try thinking keenly about its edges, its functions, its beauty, and any other aspect that crosses your thoughts. Let your mind remain focused on that particular item without looking aside for about 10 minutes. This is the best way to get ready for your meditation session.

Step 4: Pick a person that cause fear and meditate on them

Now that you have brought your thoughts into a compact state, you are ready to start meditation. Peace, love and kindness meditation is all about giving out peace love and kindness. You must visualize yourself as being the center of peace love, and kindness. In this type of meditation, you must create a beautiful world in your mind, where you are the most loving and generous person in the world. You must visualize yourself as a person who reaches out to people and tries to give them peace, love, and kindness.

To be able to deal with your negative thoughts, you must first visualize yourself extending peace, love, and kindness to the people who threaten your life. You need to bring any dangerous person in your life to your mind and start visualizing them as if they are good and beautiful people. This is the process that leads to a total change of perception and beliefs. CBT is all about changing the way you perceive people and the beliefs you have about certain things. If you can change your beliefs and perceptions, you will be on the way to finding peace and harmony. If you wish to live your life in peace and never have to worry about a person hurting your life, start giving those people love.

Extend your gestures of love to other people in society. In your meditation, try visualizing any person who is in need and just give them a gift. Through gifting such people, you put a smile on their face. Try visualizing your enemies and forgive them for all the wrongs they have done. In your mind, gift them and even give them a hug. These mental pictures will help you get rid of all your fears. You will start realizing that the people you deem as enemies are just vulnerable individuals who only need to be shown some love. They are just people who crave attention and love. If possible, you should extend your meditation gestures in real life. After meditation, try helping a person on the street. These gestures will help you learn to live a happy and fulfilling life all through.

Indeed, CBT starts with a rather straightforward way in which we can understand a challenging situation and how we react to it. What you have to remember is that cognitive behavioral therapy focuses on the three major components of a psychological problem: thoughts, emotions, and behaviors.

This simply means that when you experience a challenging situation, it is important that you break it down into these components. When you break it down in this manner, you gain clarity about where to intervene and how to do it. In other words, if there is a chain of reactions of both behavior and emotional feelings that arise from having a particular negative thought, the best approach is to go back into reexamining the thought. However, if a negative pattern of behavior seems to be the main problem, the wiser thing to do is to learn a new response to the situation.

The truth is, there is no quicker way to fix your anxiety. It takes time and commitment for you to fully overcome your fears. When you go through cognitive behavioral therapy, it is important that you face your fears head-on rather than trying to run away from them. This might make you feel worse at first, but it is only after that you can start feeling better. The most important thing is for you to try as much as you can to stick to your therapy and the advice given by your therapist.

Your pace or recovery may be slow, and this can be discouraging at the time, but you have to remember that it will be effective in the long-run. Therefore, rather than giving up, keep pressing on, and you will eventually reap the benefits. To support your therapy, it is essential that you start making positive choices. This includes everything from your level of activity to your social life and how that affects your condition. The best route is for you to begin by setting goals and making informed decisions that will boost your levels of relaxation and functionality and offer you a positive mental outlook in your daily life.

Take time to learn about your anxiety so that it becomes easier to overcome it. Education is really important in ensuring that you know what it takes to get to the other side of recovery. True, that alone will not cure your condition, but it will help you make sense of your healing therapy.

Cultivate your support network so that you are not isolated and lonely, as loneliness can make your anxiety even worse. When you establish a robust system of support from your therapist, family, and friends, you will significantly lower your level of vulnerability. Make a point to see your support group frequently so that you can share with them your worries, concerns, and progress.

Also, remember to adopt a healthy lifestyle by engaging in physical activities and eating healthy foods. This regimen goes a long way in helping to achieve relaxation by relieving tension and anxiety. Therefore, in your daily routine, make it a point to schedule regular exercises. Also, refrain from foods and drinks that may make your anxiety worse such as those containing caffeine or alcohol.

If you need to be a triumphant trader, you need to learn to deal with extreme levels of stress. The markets are regularly confused and careless; they are, with no uncertainty, stressful. Your mind has constrained resources; when you feel stressed, an extraordinary extent of your resources are dedicated to dealing with the stress. You will, in general, have little energy left with which to focus on trading. It's a great deal like "packing" for an assessment in school. It accepts twice as long to learn material when you pack. Why? This is because you are increasingly stressed when you are attempting to gain under pressure.

When you're attempting to adapt to the ferocity of the markets, you are comparably trying to perform under pressure, and under not exactly ideal conditions. As you stretch yourself as far as possible, you go through mental and emotional energy. As you go through resources, there is minimal mental and emotional energy left for trading easily, effectively, and withholding your balance. You are increasingly inclined to freeze, and may ride an emotional thrill ride as you face winning and losing trades. You may even start to freeze and act unreasonably. It's fundamental for survival, to have the option to adapt to the consistently expanding requests of the markets.

Research has demonstrated that, if you can learn satisfactory approaches to adapt to stressful circumstances, events that generally produce stress need not create the stress reaction. You can build "mental toughness". The mentally extreme individual can persevere through abnormal amounts of stressful events, yet not feel stressed out. Adapting to stress is like weightlifting. If you lift beyond what your body can physically deal with, you can harm muscle tissue. Be that as it may, if you never stretch yourself as far as possible, you'll never build up new quality. Similarly, as you build up muscles step by step, you steadily build up your capacity to deal with stress.

The essential is to know how to deal with more exceptional levels of stress, yet additionally to discover time to recover. When it comes to the markets, for instance, it's enticing to trade throughout the day, at that point work late into the night back testing and evaluating new trading systems. Be that as it may, working indefatigably at such a pace will undoubtedly destroy you eventually. It is imperative to rest and recover. That doesn't mean recoiling from the markets, yet learning to deal with the weights of the markets at a continuous, reasonable pace.

By driving yourself to more prominent levels of test, and yet resting and recovering, you can build up mental toughness similarly that a weightlifter can deal with more noteworthy and more noteworthy physical burdens.

There are some essential advances that an individual can take to plan for stress and become changed following it. To begin with, as I've expressed ordinarily, it is fundamental to get, however much rest and to unwind as could be expected. Someone who does not get the proper amount of rest have restricted mental resources to adapt to day-to-day stressful events. Getting additional rest is significant. This may mean taking arranged rests during the day to restore. Try not to wrongly think that you'll be "passing up" a trading opportunity by taking a break.

Chapter 15 Mental Thoughts

Mental toughness refers to the capability to manage, resist, and overcome any doubts, concerns, worries, and circumstances, which stop you from achieving your goals or succeeding at a particular task which you have set out to achieve.

It can also be seen as the ability to have that psychological edge which enables you to handle situations better than other people. This can be in a competition, training, or a lifestyle. It might be the ability to perform better at something or be more consistent and handle things better than your opponent. This can be measured in terms of how you remain focused, confident, determined, and in control when you are under a lot of pressure.

Mental Toughness is a Habit and a Skill

Mental toughness gives you the skills that you need to compete with other people at the highest level and to achieve the best possible potential—whether in life or sport.

It is a skill that you develop, which allows you to push through any difficult circumstances without losing your confidence or failing to achieve your goals.

There are various questions that people ask regarding mental toughness, but the major one is whether it is a skill or a habit that one is born with.

The truth is that there are various assumptions that people make when it comes to mental toughness:

- Mentally tough people usually perform better when there is pressure every time.

- Since someone falls apart when faced with stressful situations, they will tend to fall apart whenever the situation arises again.

- Mental toughness is an inborn character.

- Either a person is mentally tough, or they aren't.

The truth is that mental toughness is a skill that you can develop with time. You have to practice over it for you to be good at it. Remember that this is a skill and that skills can be developed when you put your time to it.

Mental toughness is a skill that, just like any other skill out there, can be learned. And for you to become the best at any skill you possess, you need to make it a habit. When you make something a habit, you end up making it automatic, and you won't waste a lot of time thinking how the skill works out; instead, you will make it work out for you in a short time.

The Importance of Mental Toughness in Life

Being mentally tough is a skill that will help you succeed as a person. So, let us look at the various reasons why you need to be mentally tough:

1. It Improves Your Confidence

Mentally tough people are very confident when it comes to what they do—whether in sports or their daily lives. According to studies, when your mental toughness improves, so does your confidence.

Confidence refers to a positive state of mind that allows you to have the ability to handle issues with the best outlook. When you have a proper mindset during any activity that you do, you will work at it better and with more confidence.

Whether you are working as a team member or as an individual, the only way that you can achieve your goals is to put your mind on the positive aspect of what you are doing and being able to understand what you can control or not.

Every situation usually comes with nervousness that even the best expert will experience time and time again. This nervousness is the main issue that leads to failure among people.

For you to get past this, you need to have a healthy mindset and possess mental skills with will be able to control emotions and thoughts

You need to make the goals, both short and long, your priority, and you will be able to focus on them and achieve them. When your goals are clear, you won't have the time to feel nervous at all. You will set yourself up for the ability to achieve maximum performance at any goal that you go after. For you to be mentally prepared, you need first to improve your mental toughness.

2. Greater Life Satisfaction

When you build mental strength, you gain better self-acceptance. With self, acceptance comes self-improvement. When you improve your life, you get the chance to enjoy your life fully, and you are able to turn any challenges into opportunities for you to grow.

As you build your mental strength, you will be more satisfied with your life, and you will be able to enjoy life. This is because when you are mentally strong, you have the capacity to turn your challenges into excellent opportunities.

As the mental strength grows, you will be more confident in all that you do, and you will focus on your goals and go after them. Additionally, you come up with the best priorities that are aligned better with your beliefs in life.

3. You Perform Better

The best thing that you can do as a person is to perform better at your chores. Whether you are a business person or an entrepreneur, you are out to be at your highest potential when handling any task that comes your way.

When you improve your mental strength, you will be able to reach the greatest potential ever and make sure you achieve more than you ever imagined.

Better mental strength allows you to regulate your emotions, manage your thoughts, and be more productive. This means you can focus all your energy and effort towards things that will matter the most each day.

4. You Become More Resilient

Well, it is a known fact that you cannot control everything that comes your way the way you wish to— some will make it hard for you to manage. On the other hand, what you can do is to respond better when you are faced with hard situations. When you have better mental strength, you will be able to handle any challenge that comes your way the best way possible.

Mental toughness isn't all about being strong when times are hard; instead, it is all about being able to have the mental capacity to handle situations that come your way.

Many people think that mental strength is only for hard times, but this is not true because you need to be mentally strong even when you are running typical situations in your life.

Remember, as your mental toughness improves, so does your capacity and confidence in handling any situation that comes your way.

5. It Encourages You

As an athlete or as a businessperson, you have doubts most of the time. You don't know whether you will succeed, or you will fail. When you have such doubts, you need to try and have faith while staying mentally tough. Remember, you have worked hard to develop the skills that make you mentally tough, and these skills are able to guarantee your success.

You need to trust this training when you go out to do something. Make sure you work with your teammates and other people so that you overcome any challenge that arises.

As you realize the need to remain mentally tough, your mental state becomes an asset in any task that you handle.

6. Improves Work Outcome

Studies show that mental toughness is a big factor when determining the outcomes in organizations. People who are mentally tough handle situations better than those that aren't tough at all. This is why it is better to have workers that are mentally tough on your team rather than have those that aren't.

Mentally tough people tend to deliver more work in such a short time, and they also work purposefully towards their goals each day. They are also more competitive, and this means better output, better attendance, and meeting deadlines.

7. More Work Satisfaction

Mentally tough people handle stress better and are less likely to develop mental problems when at work. They also handle stress well and are less prone to being bullied.

They are also more positive and will handle any work you throw at them the best way, regardless of the challenges that they will experience, they also respond better to adversity and change, which means that new ideas will be adopted better compared to people who are mentally weak.

They, therefore, are able to contribute to the organization in a better way compared to other people.

8. It Eliminates Self-doubt

Whether your goal is to finish the marathon, or to double revenue, you will usually experience self-doubt in one way or the other. Having doubts about the goals you have, and how to achieve them forms a common issue that people go through in their quest to attain something.

When you have the mental toughness that comes with training and practice, you will be able to eliminate any negative talk and go for your goal with better confidence.

9. It Gives You Motivation

Organizations around the world are faced with the problem of how to keep their workers motivated. However, mentally tough people have the capacity to stick to their goals and stay motivated. Mental toughness will help you focus on the goal and then go after it, even when you don't have the strength to do so.

You will be able to find your inner strength, especially when you feel unambitious, tired, and discouraged.

10. Helps You Stick to Your Values

Mentally strong people know good advice when they see it. When you are going after a goal, bad advice usually tends to drown out anything good that you are going after, which is why you need to be able to filter out the bad and go for the good.

When you are mentally tough, you have the capacity to rule out any bad criticisms and advice from the people that are around you, and you can focus on the good things.

You will be focused and follow your values to the latter, and this, in turn, helps you make the best decisions regardless of the feedback that you receive from the people that are around you.

11.   Helps You Learn From Mistakes

Many people hide their mistakes, and this increases the probability that you will end up making the mistakes again sooner than you think. When you are mentally tough, you will be able to accept any responsibility that comes with making mistakes then be able to learn from those mistakes.

12.   With every lesson that you learn, you will be moving closer to achieving your goal.

While mistakes lead to failure, and failure is the core ingredient in losing out on your goal, when you make a mistake, you need to learn to spring back. People that are mentally tough have high self-esteem and will be able to bounce back from failure better than before. Failure is not a reason to give up for these people; instead, it is a way to move closer to their success.

13.   Helps You Manage Your Fears

When you step out of your comfort zone, you find it hard to do some things that you were used to. When you are mentally tough, you get the courage to face and handle your fears better. Strong people have the ability to tolerate high levels of discomfort and will be able to move forward.

Chapter 16 Characteristics of Mentally Though People

All mentally tough people have developed specific characteristics that are helpful to how they think, react, and make important decisions. Studying these characteristics and making attempts to mimic the behaviors and thinking patterns is one sure way to reach your goal of mental toughness faster. Use it as a blueprint that can be used and reused at will. Over time, the process will become like second-nature. You will instantly know when you are falling back into old habits or behaviors and can correct the course.

Ability to Make Non-Emotional Choices

Allowing an emotional state to dictate your decision-making process will skew your outcome in directions that are non-productive or harmful. No matter how much your small child wants to cross a busy street by themselves and offer a tantrum to try and force a decision in their favor, better sense usually prevails, and the child waits until a responsible person can help them navigate heavy traffic safely. Letting emotions drive the decision can have terrible consequences, depending on the situation. Learn to separate emotion from sensible, rational thoughts.

See the reality of the situation

Raw emotions can paint colors onto a canvas, which are not truly a part of the landscape. Irrational fears, negative thoughts, and a generalized feeling of hopelessness can invade every time you are faced with having to make an emotionally laced decision. As difficult as it may seem, take time to calmly look at the situation with an eye for realism.

Goal-Driven

Keeping your eye on the goal is an important part of the development of mental toughness and a standard characteristic of anyone that always seems to achieve everything they set out to do or attain. It is an admirable quality worth replicating as often as possible.

Recognizing a dead-end road

Taking the wrong path or making incorrect decisions is a waste of valuable time, resources, and energy. The skills it takes to recognize a dead-end road before you take the plunge is priceless. Is it a road filled with potholes or other unsavory obstacles? Is there a smoother, more direct route available? Not every path in life need be a struggle. At times, the struggles experienced are due to poor decision-making. Step back and look at the big picture. Even a difficult hedge-maze is solvable by looking at it from above.

Untethering from details

Details can keep you bogged down, much like the tethers that hold back a hot air balloon from its flight. It is important to address all the details but do not get hung up in the process. Keep pushing forward for positive results. Maintain flexibility to change things if it makes the process easier. Higher levels of success are possible if you refrain from boxing yourself into side compartments and hop down unnecessary rabbit holes. Keep your eye on the goal line.

Keeping a finished vision in mind

Knowing you have completed a road trip is obvious once you have reached your desired destination. An important characteristic of those with mental toughness is the ability to keep the finished goal or vision in mind, no matter what mayhem and chaos happens. It sounds easier than when you are stuck in the situation. The skill of practically putting on blinders to avoid being affected by the emotions of others is one that will serve you well. Stay in the knowledge that reaching your goal often means making unpleasant decisions or ones that are not popular with everyone in your circle.

Ability to Set Aside Stress and Emotion

Stress can get kicked into high gear during emotional situations and exchanges. Decision-making and solutions can become clouded when stress is in a peak amount. Become instantly tougher in mental processes by learning how to set stress and emotional entanglement aside. You need a clearing, devoid of pressure to have the best perspective on any given situation.

Ability to Welcome Change and Remain Flexible

When companies downsize or restructure, employees are faced with job loss, and this can sometimes be devastating. A mentally strong person will seize the opportunity to improve their life by weighing all of their options. If a mentally strong person who had been considering a career change is suddenly faced with losing their job, he or she will take this time to develop their skill set, return to school, or polish their resume to make a career change.

Refuse to Let Fear Hold Them Back

A mentally tough person does not let fear hold them back. Everyone must go through challenges in life, and it is how we view those challenges that can shape our lives for the better. Change is scary, but so is remaining in the same stagnant situation indefinitely. A mentally tough person would rather be scared for a short amount of time while they are going through a change in life than live in fear of the change, never improving or bettering their situation.

Will Not Let Toxic People Affect Them

A toxic person is someone who ruins the environment or the atmosphere for those around them. The toxic person might be incredibly jealous, judgmental, or just negative overall. A toxic person is like the grown-up version of the playground bully: he or she has low self-esteem and is so unhappy with their own lives, so they are constantly trying to bring others down to their level. A mentally strong person realizes this and will do their best to see things from the toxic person's point of view if possible. A mentally strong person also realizes that the toxic person is unhappy, so he or she will not let the toxic opinions and attitude affect them and their work.

Exert Assertiveness

A mentally strong person is assertive. They say what they mean, and they mean what they say. They know how to use concise language so that the meaning of their words is not mistaken and their intentions are not taken the wrong way. Mentally strong people know how to say no. They know that it's ok to take time to themselves, whether that means saying no to an invitation they don't want to accept or simply staying in on a Saturday night to recharge. Mentally strong people also know when to set boundaries.

They are very confident

If you don't feel confident about yourself and your skills, you cannot expect someone else to feel confident about you. Real confidence is essential and not false bravado. People often tend to mask their insecurities by merely projecting confidence, instead of being confident. A confident person will always stand apart when compared to all those who are indecisive, doubtful, and skittish. Their confidence often inspires others as well.

They are good at neutralizing toxic people

A mentally tough person can keep his or her emotions in check while confronting a toxic person. Their approach would often be rational. If you want to be mentally strong, then you should be able to identify negative emotions like anger and shouldn't let these feelings get the better of you.

They can say no

If you want to reduce your chances of experiencing stress and depression, then learn to say "no." Saying "no" is, in fact, good for your mental health. All those who are mentally tough possess the self-esteem and the foresight that helps them say no. If you have trouble saying "no" to others, then you should start working on it immediately. Saying "no" not only helps you in avowing unnecessary burden, but it will also help you in prioritizing your work and cutting off toxic people from your life.

They can embrace failure

Failures are very common, and everyone has their fair share of failures in their lives. Mentally tough people are capable of embracing their failures. No one can experience success without knowing what failure is. When you can acknowledge that you are on the wrong path, are aware of the mistakes you are making, and can embrace your failures, only then will you be able to achieve success.

They exercise

Exercising can help you in finding mental, physical, and emotional stability. When you start exercising, you are not only improving your physical health, you are getting rid of negative emotions as well. Start exercising at least thrice a week and you will feel better about yourself. Your self-esteem will get a healthy boost when you can develop your physical image. A person who is mentally tough knows the importance of exercising and will make sure that they are getting their quota of exercise daily. The endorphin high that you experience after exercising can lend your perspective some much-needed positivity.

They get sufficient sleep

Sleep is quite essential if you are trying to improve your mental toughness. While you are sleeping, your brain starts working on removing all the toxic proteins that are produced because of the neural activity that takes place while you are awake. Well, your brain can do this only when you are asleep.

They are always positive

Reading news these days has become a sad affair. Mass killings, suicide bombings, violence, crippling economies, failing companies, and plenty of environmental mishaps. Phew, that is a lot of negativity to go through. In times like these, it is quite easy to give up on a positive attitude. A mentally tough person wouldn't worry about all that for a simple reason. He or she cannot control any of those things. However, their attitude is something that they can control, and that's what they would concentrate on. They wouldn't waste their energies on something that cannot be helped. Instead, try utilizing your energy to do something good, and it might be helpful.

Mental toughness isn't a quality that only a few are blessed with. You can achieve it with some effort.

Chapter 17 Scientific Studies of Mentally Tough

Most scientists stand out in their career than others simply because they have a diehard mentality that is very tough at discovering something new. A scientist who is not interested in discovering something new will always need to depend on what is already existing, but the one who is inspired and spirited will always desire to invent something, he wants something new to give to the world, something that nobody has ever done.

From history, we have seen scientist who gave us what we are still using today, such as, the principle of developing the LED globe and electricity. Michael Faraday the man who discovered electricity based on a particular principle of electricity he found out through personal discovery, Thomas Edison, the man who discovered the electric bulb tried several times and failed but he never gave up and he ended up giving the world one of the greatest discoveries of man which principle is today the basis of LED electric bulb production. Again, one thing that is common among these men was mental strength, if Thomas Edison gave up his idea on electric bulb, then he would never have discovered it. Mental toughness is the ability to consistently stick to what you believe that is going to work based on experimenting when it comes to scientific discovery.

Many scientists continue to experiment on something until they see that it is going to work, if it doesn't work, they keep on trying until finally they get the result. At this level, this is the scientists' mental toughness, the believe in the positive result of the outcome of what they are inventing. We can also borrow the knowledge of the science way of thinking or mentality to develop the area of life which we found is near impossible to achieve, I'll rather believe that it is going to work, and I'll keep working at it until I get it right.

The only thing that makes it not working for now is simply because you have not gotten it right, and the only way you'll ever get it right is when you keep working it and keep on practicing and doing it till you get it right.

The story of Thomas Edison is very interesting, he kept on believing that his invention will work, he never doubted himself, at the point of giving up, he just discovered what was missing and when he did discovered it, the rest is history, he got it right at that moment, the pain and suffering over the failed attempts was forgotten and what he achieve was what no man ever did achieve, today Thomas Edison is one of the renowned scientist for his good works of discovering the electric bulb.

The difference is that these men continued consistently believing that what they are doing will work and it did work. You will not just believe but add what you are doing to what you believe. With the right believe system that 'it is going to work' and actually doing what you believe is what will give you the result not when you don't believe in what you are doing, that will not give you the right result.

Again a man said during the time of Aristotle, the great Greek philosopher, that man cannot fly, Aristotle opined rather that man will fly, he believed in what he said, but many people mocked him and in response they said to him "You ought to know that you are wrong, even the ostrich with wings cannot fly, why should you ever conceive in your mind that man without wings will fly?" and so nobody believe what he said.

But many years later, man is flying from country to country from one continent to the other and from earth to the moon and outer space. Actually those who usually believe have a better mental strength or toughness than others.

Mental toughness also has to do with what you believe, if you believe in something and you develop a passion for it, you work towards achieving it, you will definitely get that thing. For this has been the story of many people in time past.

Chapter 18 Understanding Fear

Fear is nuclear fuel in a human activity reactor. It forces one to act in the way that no threats, persuasion, logical arguments or arguments work.

Fear is a powerful resource, proven in business more than once. Who does not know J? Welch, the one who, having become the head of General Electric, reformed the company, using the fear of employees to be dismissed? Of course, fear was not the only force in his managerial revolution, but one of the main ones. J. Welch was not afraid of change, resolutely got rid of indecisive managers, and introduced the now-famous principle of working with staff up or out. He received his nickname Neutron Jack for dismissing about 100,000 people from the company. The management method of J. Welch was compared with an iron hand in a velvet glove. In August 1984, Fortune magazine, making a rating of the most severe bosses of America, put Welch on the first line.

When subordinates are reliably protected from coarse and direct threats, the manager may use more subtle ways of instilling fear. How did, for example, the company Ohio Bell, do this? Here they simply showed a film to all employees, who modeled the future. In this imagined future, Congress intended to nationalize the telephone system, as it gradually went bankrupt and lost its ability to provide relevant services. As a result, a huge number of employees lost their jobs. The film ended with the text that the announcer read to the audience: "Full-time work for a full day's pay! This appeal would help save the company if many years ago, workers followed it." The company calculated that the increase in labor productivity after watching this film allowed it to increase its revenues by $ 29 million over three years. A good argument for using fear to increase business profitability!

So, if we decided to use the emotion of fear in business development, how can this be done correctly?

We know for sure that fear affects not only the psyche, but also the entire body, the work of the endocrine glands are activated, and adrenaline is released into the blood. A person can only follow two primitive instincts - to face danger and attack first or escape. Fear can be rational, justified (when we are dealing with a real threat) and irrational (neurotic). In any case, our body acts the same way. The development of a sense of fear (emotion) occurs in two neural paths that must function simultaneously. The neurons process information, it is with their help that the body's responses (reflexes) to external and internal stimuli are formed. The first path is responsible for generating the most important emotions, the reaction along this path occurs quickly, allowing us to almost immediately respond to signs of danger. On the second path, the reaction is slower but more accurate. It allows you to more accurately assess the circumstances and more correctly respond to danger.

Since fear is learned and remembered the response of an organism to a threat (existing or imaginary), it means that this reaction can be controlled and even prevented or neutralized.

However, as a manager who worked with professional boxers, once said: "Both the hero and the coward feel fear equally, but only the hero struggles with his fear and turns him into a desire to win." Add: it is developed emotional intelligence that turns fear into a victorious resource.

Fear: disassemble, understand, use

We learn to use emotions to increase the efficiency of our business. To begin, consider the typical "recommendation for use" for fear. Naturally, first for personal use.

Recommendation 1. Get rid of.

If it is necessary to free oneself from fear, then one of the most powerful means is the opposite action. There is an opportunity - do what you fear. Afraid of heights - jump with a parachute, afraid of negotiations - participate in them constantly! This is possible if you overcome yourself.

Another classic piece of advice is to laugh at your fears, make them funny and funny. An annoying (frightening) senior business partner can be thought of as a monument along which pigeon droppings flow, for example. An employee of the tax police will not be afraid if you present him in a rage running after you with a fly swatter, etc. It has been established that laughter has a startling effect not only on mental processes but also on physiological processes. It suppresses pain, as catecholamine and endorphins are released during laughter. The former prevents inflammation, the latter acts as morphine. Laughter reduces stress and its effects, reducing the concentration of stress hormones - norepinephrine, cortisol, and dopamine. And more importantly: the positive effect of laughter persists throughout the day!

Recommendation 2. Understand.

A thinking person is less afraid. He is simply ... not in a hurry to be afraid, he has a habit developed on his machine that he will first understand what is happening and whether there are serious reasons for concern. This removes all sorts of fear and other empty experiences.

Recommendation 3. Act.

Reasonable actions calm the one who is anxious and change the situation itself to a more prosperous one. In a dangerous situation it is important not to worry, but to act correctly. Remember, the movie "The Crew," the ship's commander, summarizes: "To stay here is to die. So, you need to take off, no matter how small the chances for this are!" The commander does not have the right to fear in a dangerous situation.

Recommendation 4. Recall all good.

Fear leaves when a successful, positive experience appears when a person has confidence that he is able to cope with difficulties, that he is a winner. Gather your positive experience and accumulate success, as the camel accumulates water in his hump. Useful in a particularly dry period.

Recommendation 5. Raise your own morale.

How do warriors raise morale before a battle? The battle cry "Hurray!" How do Tibetan monks lead themselves to a meditative state? Sing the mantra "om." Each of us can find words, phrases that drive away fear and change our state. For example:

✓ "I'll do it!"

✓ "Yes!"

✓ "I!"

✓ "We will rock you!"

✓ "Forward, forward, forward!"

You shouldn't sag under a changeable world, let it be better bent under us!

It is important to select phrases individually, exclusively for yourselves. They do not necessarily need speaking out loud, they will produce the same effect if they are spoken yourself. The phrase with a built-in melody that can be sung even more strongly. In personal stock, it is good to have several phrases for the same state. If one does not work, the other will work.

Look for your own verbal formulas that are perfect for you. Although if someone's ready-made phrase works for you, why refuse a gift? For example, the phrase "I am not a hundred dollar bill to please everyone" helped out and continues to help many.

Recommendation 6. Fantasize.

Sometimes fear arises from a collision with something new, unusual, incomprehensible. Everything new in one degree or another causes wariness, apprehension. This is how the instinct of self-preservation works. After all, the unknown can be fraught with danger or even a threat to life! Fantasy helps to cope with this. It is not known what to expect from the negotiations. Are you nervous? Imagine unfamiliar business partners in suits and ties in an unusual situation. Let in your imagination they suddenly take out shopping bags with rotten eggs and tomatoes and begin to throw them in your direction. And you dodge them dexterously ... Then you take out a baseball bat and start to beat those tomatoes back! Spin the absurdity of this situation to the limit, until you feel funny and easy. Humor, as we know, is the best cure for fear.

Chapter 19 Mentally Stronger and Acting Tough

There is a significant difference between acting tough and being mentally strong. A controlling supervisor at work, an incredibly demanding boss, bossy co-worker, or even an aggressive customer might be masking their lack of mental toughness by putting up a façade of toughness. Acting might help in improving someone's success initially, but not forever. However, for how long can a person keep faking? Mental strength is essential in the long run, and it cannot be faked. A successful person didn't rise to the top by feigning toughness. Instead, their success is associated with their mental strength. The stronger they are, the higher are their chances to succeed. Grit and persistence are necessary to become a top performer in any avenue. Along with this, there needs to be a desire to keep improving.

1: Failure isn't an option. Or is it?

It is highly unlikely that you will always be successful. Failure is a part of achieving success. Striving for success is a healthy attitude, but if you start believing that you always need to succeed on the first attempt itself, you are setting yourself up for failure. A mentally tough person knows that failures are part and parcel of life. They would think of failure as a temporary setback that they need to overcome and with this positive attitude, they will be able to do so quite quickly. A person who is pretending to be tough will be of the opinion that a failure is never an option. This attitude can become quite problematic when things don't go their way.

A perfect example of this is in relationships. How many times have you asked a person out, only to be turned down? This is something that happens to everyone. How you respond to rejection, however, defines whether you are acting tough or truly mentally strong. If you are merely acting tough you won't accept being rejected. Instead, you will likely keep asking the person out over and over again, believing that they will eventually give in, and thus make you the winner. This might happen in movies from time to time. However, in real life, constantly bothering a person can get you into real trouble. In fact, it could result in that person taking a restraining order out on you, turning a simple failure into an absolute catastrophe.

When you are mentally tough you will respond in a very different way. Rather than refusing to take "no" for an answer you will accept the outcome and consider your options. You might ask around to see why you were rejected. Perhaps the person you asked out is in a relationship, or maybe they just broke up with someone and need some time alone. In these cases you might choose to bide your time and try again later. Or maybe the person doesn't know you well enough to accept your invitation. In this case you can invest the time and effort to get to know them better, thereby improving your chances later. It may, however, simply be that they aren't interested in you, in which case you can move on and look for love elsewhere, not letting this rejection affect you any more than it should.

2: Faking toughness to mask insecurities

When a person tries to act tough, he or she is trying on a fake persona that seems to say "Hey! Look at me! I am great!" The façade they put up is quite brittle, and it can crumble at any given point of time. That tough exterior is simply a tool to hide their insecurities. It is okay to have certain vulnerabilities; you are human after all. A mentally strong person is aware of his or her vulnerabilities and tries to work on fixing them instead of pretending that they don't exist. You will be able to progress if you try fixing any weaknesses instead of covering them up and then hoping that they will go away.

One of the most common signs that a person is acting tough is that they appear to be far more self-confident than a normal person would be. This is often seen in confrontational situations. Any time two people get into an argument that gets out of control you will inevitably hear one of them begin to boast about not being afraid to fight. The lines "You don't scare me" or "I know martial arts" or "I'm going to destroy you" often hide the truth, namely that the person is in fact terrified of getting into a fight because they know they would lose. Therefore, the axiom "The dog who barks the most bites the least" comes into play here.

Alternatively, a mentally strong person won't boast that they aren't afraid, nor will they proclaim any fighting abilities that they might have. In fact, a truly mentally strong person will gladly walk away from a confrontation whenever possible. This is especially true for anyone who is trained in fighting. Since they are confident in their abilities they don't have the need to impress anyone or prove themselves in any way.

Instead, they keep their composure and dictate the course of events as a result.

3: The "I can do anything" attitude

Being self-confident is important. However, there is a fine line between being self-confident and being cocky or overconfident. Self-confidence will help you in tackling challenging situations, and overconfidence is your shortcut to disappointments and failures. Overestimating your abilities will leave you inadequately equipped for dealing with realities of lie and underestimating the time required for achieving your goals will lead to severe disappointments. Mental strength is about understanding where you stand and what your abilities are. It isn't about having a false sense of bravado that can crack under the slightest pressures. It is about understanding your skills and working hard for achieving the goals you have set for yourself.

Someone who claims to be able to do anything will likely take on tasks or projects that are beyond their abilities just to impress others. This can be especially true in the event that a person takes a job that they aren't suited for. Any job requires a certain level of experience, training and inherent ability. As a result, when a person lacks those things they will struggle and likely fail. A person who acts tough will hide their lack of skill sets with the boast that they can do anything, regardless of what it is. More often than not the result is disastrous, as the individual gets into a situation that they simply cannot handle.

Alternatively, a mentally strong person will reveal any concerns they have before taking on a job or a role that they feel they aren't qualified for. More often than not they will simply turn an offer down, citing their lack of experience as the reason for doing so. However, in the event that they accept the challenge they will seek out as much training and support as possible. This will help them to learn the skills they need in order to be successful in the task at hand. Additionally, by looking to others for support they can get real time solutions for the problems they face, thus enabling them to learn as they go without risking their success or the success of those relying on them.

4: Acting tough usually involves a lot of pride
Those who would want to be perceived as being tough always feel that they have something to prove to others. Their self-worth depends on what others think of them. It doesn't depend on their perception of

themselves but on what the world thinks of them. An attitude like this can take a toll on the individual. If your happiness is dependent on someone else's opinion, then you can never be satisfied. Becoming mentally tough is all about learning to be humble and understanding your abilities. A person who is mentally strong won't hesitate in asking for help when the need arises. They won't let pride stop them from asking for help or admitting ignorance of something.

An example of this toxic pride can be found in a person's need to be better than everyone else. It is perfectly healthy and normal to be competitive, but only to a point. When a person is acting tough they take being competitive to a whole new level. In business, when a person absolutely needs to be first in sales, customer service results or any other area where performance can be measured it indicates that they are trying to prove a point, namely that they are the best. The need to prove this usually indicates the opposite, namely that the individual has low self esteem and is trying to compensate for it.

In contrast, someone who is mentally strong will appreciate the times when they are first in areas of measurable performance, such as sales, customer service, etc. However, they will never rely on that rank. Instead, they will usually attribute it to luck, the effort of the team or some other phenomenon that downplays their personal role in the success. Furthermore, they will be the first one to congratulate someone else who earns first place in those areas. Rather than envying another person's success they will celebrate it, offering true support and encouragement as a result.

5: "Tough" people tend to ignore their emotions

Concealing emotions is possible for a while. However, this isn't a viable idea in the long run. Ignoring feelings, in the long run, can cause a lot of damage to your mental health. Suppressed emotions tend to wiggle their way to the surface, eventually if not immediately. Not acknowledging your emotions and hoping that they will pass will not do you any good whatsoever. Being strong is all about understanding your emotions and acting rationally after considering those emotions. A person who is acting tough often believes that emotions are a sign of weakness and tends to ignore them. Only if you acknowledge what you feel, will you be able to get control over it.

This can often be seen in circumstances when a person has their feelings hurt, either by an event or a person, but they refuse to admit that they are adversely affected in any way. When a person acting tough is overlooked for a promotion they will likely proclaim that they didn't care about the promotion anyway. They may even go as far as to say that they are better off without it, and that it is something only an idiot would want. The problem with this is that they downplay important things in life, which leads to them not going the extra mile to achieve the goals they really want. Rather than using the pain of a situation as inspiration to improve, they simply hide the pain and remain stagnant.

Someone who is mentally tough will know the value of emotions, especially negative ones. By embracing the hurt of being passed over for a job or a promotion they find the will to improve their chances for the next opportunity that comes along. This can also be seen in athletes who use losing to spur them on in training so that they can run faster in the next race. The bottom line is that a mentally strong person will wear their heart on their sleeve so that they remain committed to doing whatever it takes to become successful.

6: They thrive on power

All those who act like they are tough, decide to do so because they like being perceived as powerful and in control. Due to this, they often tend to micromanage and boss others around. They also end up having unreasonable expectations and demands. A person who is mentally strong will like to focus their energy on controlling their thoughts and rationalizing their behavior instead of trying to control all other external factors.

This can be seen all too often in the world of retail where those who act tough fool themselves into positions of authority all the time. Any time someone who acts tough gets into a managerial position they turn their responsibility into power. They see their promotion as a prize, something they don't have to work for any more. Subsequently, they tend to become lazier and lazier, delegating more and more work to those under their supervision. Any time they make a decision that is questionable they fall back on their position, reminding people that they are the boss and that what they say goes.

A mentally strong person demonstrates a completely different character when they are in positions of authority. Rather than viewing a promotion as the prize they see it as a challenge, an opportunity to prove their worth all over again. The result is that they increase their efforts, working harder than ever to ensure their own success as well as the success of those under their supervision. Additionally, a mentally strong person welcomes other opinions and viewpoints, drawing from the vision and experience of others to ensure the best choices are made each and every time.

7: Acting tough = Tolerating pain

Becoming mentally tough isn't about tolerating pain. It is about learning from the pain you experience so that you don't have to go through the same thing again. A mentally strong person would like to focus on their overall growth and development and wouldn't treat their body like a machine.

It is not about having a tough exterior, but it is about having a healthy mind that doesn't waver easily. It is about developing mental strength and like any other exercise, it takes practice to improve mental strength.

Associating toughness with the ability to tolerate pain can also be seen in the workplace environment. Everyone goes through the scenario where they find themselves in a job that they begin to hate. The difference is what a person does when they come to the realization that they are fed up with their job and want a better one. Someone who acts tough will remain in the job they hate, believing that they are demonstrating strength by enduring their day to day suffering. In their eyes the longer they remain is the stronger they are. This means that rather than trying to improve their life they simply strive to tolerate the emotional pain their circumstances create.

Alternatively, a mentally strong person will recognize that pain is a sign that something is wrong and change is required. Needless to say, this isn't about the pain associated with growing and developing, such as weight training or developing a new skill, rather this is the pain associated with hitting your thumb with a hammer. You can choose to embrace the pain, or you can choose to stop hitting your thumb with a hammer. A mentally strong person will choose the second option, seeking a different job or a transfer that will end the pain they experience in the job they have. In the end, mentally strong people know that it's not about putting on a brave face when facing harmful situations, rather it's about avoiding harmful situations whenever possible.

Chapter 17 Comfort Zone: What and Find the Comfort Zone

Many psychologists and scientists have used the word 'Comfort Zone' to mean many different things. Some say it is a time, a place, a space or a happening in a person's life where he is most comfortable. Comfort zone is all of this and more. It is a routine, a behavior, a habit, an activity and even an overall way of life that doesn't feel stressful. It is something that somehow gives a person mental and emotional security. It can also give a person a steady dose of happiness and a sense of contentment.

Given these definitions of a comfort zone, it does not sound like a really bad thing to have, does it? In fact, it sounds like something everyone wants to attain. A comfort zone is not really a bad thing. What really makes it awful is when a person is living in a comfort zone for too long.

As earlier mentioned, having a comfort zone is not bad. The thing that makes it unfavorable is when a person gets stuck in it for so long. Being stuck in the comfort zone for so long can make a person lazy, unmotivated and, often, frustrated. He also becomes less productive and his performance is not as great as it used to be.

Experts believe that there should be some stress or anxiety in a person's life. This kind of anxiety is called the 'Optimal Anxiety'. It is called as such because it is not too stressful that a person gets a nervous breakdown, yet it is not so easy that the person remains in his comfort zone. This kind of anxiety is when stress levels are just a bit higher than normal. It also has to be something that's just outside the comfort zone.

An example of an optimal stress for a student is his final exam. For employees, this can be likened to deadlines, performance evaluations, and job interviews. These kinds of stresses are not considered as life and death situations and keep people on their toes.

How Hard is It to Leave The Comfort Zone?

Have you ever tried breaking a 10 year habit like quitting smoking? If the answer is yes, the reason why leaving the comfort zone is hard will be very relatable. Comfort zones give people some form of happiness and contentment. It is very hard to leave because why would anyone want to leave something that makes him happy? Why would anyone risk going out and venturing into the world where he can be criticized, judged and ultimately FAIL? People do not like leaving their comfort zones because they have gotten used to it.

These are some of the other reasons why leaving the comfort zone is difficult:

1. It is easy – leaving something that takes very little effort and gives them comfort and security is not something that many people would do. People in the comfort zone see it as something effortless that gives them all the satisfaction they crave. It provides them with security, satisfaction, and comfort. Leaving something that does not require a lot of effort on their part but yields an acceptable result can be tough.

2. They are afraid of the unknown – some people have this irrational fear of the unknown while others thrive in not knowing what will happen next. The people in the former situation are the ones who want to keep staying in their comfort zone because they are afraid of what will happen if they leave. They fear that venturing into the unknown will just bring chaos in their life. They stick

to their comfort zone because they know what to do in that situation.

3. They are afraid of failure and getting rejected – people who stay in the comfort zone hate knowing that they have failed or that they are being rejected. They stay in the comfort zone because it is a state where they are always accepted. They almost never encounter failure when they are in the comfort zone. They use the comfort zone to be protected from potential failures and rejection like a security blanket.

4. It is predictable – some people thrive on routines and predictability and do not like to venture into something that can result to unpredictable outcomes. These routines and repetitive events provide comfort knowing that the next part of the 'story' of their lives will unfold just as they thought it would. They dislike surprises and prefer things to happen as expected.

5. They feel like they have control – Many people who stay in the comfort zone think that they are taking control of their life by steering it away from potential disasters. They think that they would not be affected by any outside force if they just stick to their routine. The

predictability once again feels desirable when people feel like they are losing control over the situation.

6. It is their form of normal – people who have been stuck in their comfort zone think that being in that situation means normal. They see other things as outside the box and unusual if they stray away from routine and predictability.

7. They dislike change – this is not to say that they are rigid and unbendable, but sometimes, people stay in their comfort zones simply because they hate changes. They like the idea that things will stay the same no matter what happens.

To reiterate, having a comfort zone is neither a good thing nor a bad thing. It is when a person remains in the comfort zone for too long that makes it awful. When people start becoming predictable and the excitement for life is gone, that's when it goes bad.

Getting out of the comfort zone has many benefits that far outweigh all the reasons why people do not want to leave it. These benefits enrich and uplift the lives of anyone who take the leap and try the unknown.

Chapter 18 How to Develop Habits and Set the Right Goals

Transformative habits are habits that you can employ in your everyday life that greatly aid growth. Adopting these habits and putting them to work in your life will put you on the right track to learn all there is to learn about something, to use it to its fullest, and to have an endlessly renewable interest in that subject.

Let's take a look at five transformative habits to keep when learning about something. You will want to write these down somewhere and make active strides toward integrating them into your daily routine!

1. Have a burning passion.

Go into the area of your interest with a passion for learning more about it. Let that passion carry you through the following steps. The more of a desire you have to know more about the subject and the more passionate you are about making this a part of your life, the more able you will be to face the bumps in the road.

People who perform the best are the people who love what they do. As a result of that love for what they do, they spend time and energy on it that everyone cheering them on will never see. Being devoted to your craft means more than simply being there when others can see you.

Take the lead, stay interested in your passion, and develop a passion for being the best at what you do.

2. Dream big.

The dreams we have for the future are what keep us working hard and running toward the horizon. Knowing that bigger and better things wait for us on the other side of the hurdles we face is a huge motivator that will help us to smash through those hurdles. There is nothing wrong with aiming for the stars with the goals that you set. They will only serve to help you.

As you find your dreams set on higher and higher goals, you will find that your acumen and your skill will continue to grow to support those goals. These things are connected and aspiring to be more does have a massive effect on your growth and development.

3. Be disciplined enough to do the mundane daily tasks.

Being dedicated to a craft, job, task, hobby, sport, etc., means more than being present for the parts that others will see. It means being there for more than just the fun parts, the glory, the excitement, and the joy. It means being there for the mundane, boring, tedious, grinding parts of it as well.

Honing a skill or a craft takes hours upon hours of practice, failure, adjustment, practice, failure, adjustment, practice... It goes on and on and you have to be ready to be there for that.

Self-discipline is a huge part of success in general. If you can have the control over yourself to do what needs to be done, when it needs to be done, you have a better chance of reaching unimaginable success.

4. Be willing to be coached.

This is really important, so pay close attention: no one ever learned anything by acting like they already understood it. Be willing to be taught, be willing to learn, be willing to be corrected, be willing to be corrected, and always be on the lookout for new information on the subject of your interest.

There is no shortage of information on any topic you care to learn, no matter what it is. There is always a way to learn something you want to learn.

The most crucial point is to be willing to let someone teach you something. No one will think less of you for the questions you ask when learning your skills. If you let your pride get the better of you while you're learning your craft however, you will lose the respect of others, as well as their support. You will also be cutting yourself off at the knees as regards further improvement or honing of skills.

5. Desire to be challenged.

Once you allow the challenging aspects of your craft to leave the area, you will lose interest. The best way to keep a muscle toned is to flex it, right? Think of your brain like the muscle it is. It needs to be worked and challenged and exercised in order to retain what it's learned its elasticity, and its ability to make things work!

Setting challenges and goals for yourself can give you things to work toward and it can keep your interest fresh! Remember that if there is no one with whom you can be in competition, you can always be in competition with your former self. There is always room for you to improve, and you should be eager to take that opportunity!

While we're on the subject of habits, there are some habits that could benefit you as someone who is looking to succeed. These are known as the habits of effective people. They are the habits that, if you keep them, they'll keep you on the right track and primed for success!

Let's take a look at those habits now.

1. Don't work yourself to death.

Striving for a sustainable lifestyle in which you can get all your work done, while still affording adequate time to take care of yourself is the most important thing.

If you can achieve this, you can ensure that you will be effective in the long term. This is a sustainable, recuperative, and rechargeable approach that allows you to take the time to do the things you personally need to do. Work is not your entire life and you would do well to treat it that way!

2. Be proactive.

Getting out ahead of things is always a great idea. Don't live your life hopping from urgent task to urgent task. Take the time to look ahead, see what will be needed in the near future, and account for it. This will leave you with fewer fires to put out, so to speak.

Have a clear vision for what your future should be and systematically work toward it to bring it into being!

3. Have your ending in mind from the start.

If you know where you're going, you can more accurately decide what you should be doing right now. Working right now, for the sake of working right now, is a waste of your time and your effort. You need to be sure that what you're doing will ultimately lead you where you want to go.

4. Prioritize

It can be easy to get snowed under with all the things that lay before you, ready to be done. In order to stave off that panic, the most efficient thing to do is prioritize. Find the things that need to come first and get a jump on them. As you systematically work through the things that need to get done right now, you will find yourself rolling into the future and setting up tasks that will need to be done later.

It's is imperative to be able to differentiate between urgent and important. Something could have a timestamp on it that tells you it needs to get done right now. However, it might be something that you can delegate, or it might not be important to you at all to complete. Be sure to factor this into your evaluation before you start working on it.

5. Keep it fair.

When you're looking at the outcome of any arrangement that you're looking to make, don't try to come out on top. Coming out on top is a concept that movie villains use, and it doesn't actually do anyone any actual good. Through litigation and the trouble it takes to manipulate people into these situations, it's not even worth it in the end.

Go into partnerships and arrangements with the idea that they are mutually beneficial for both of you. If you can achieve that, you're doing great. Having an honest mindset when you go into business with someone is the best way to make sure you're both getting what you need from the business and that nothing will go awry.

6. Hear before being heard.

Be sure that when you're being presented with a problem, you do your best to hear all there is to be said about it, from as many angles as are available. Once you have all the information, you can throw in your input and go from there to reach a resolution.

If you jump in too quickly in an effort to be heard, you could discourage someone from coming forward, you could muddy the perception of what occurred, it could stir the pot, and you might be missing out on pertinent information that could more easily help you to reach a resolution.

Be willing to hear others before insisting that you be heard.

7. Synergize.

This is a very popular word that is used throughout business and strategy. Let's breakdown what it is and what it means. Synergy is the interaction or cooperation of two or more assets to produce a combined result or effect that is greater than the sum of their individual parts or effects.

If you are able to put your sense of self-gratification aside so that you and your colleagues can share in the success, you will find the success to be even greater in measure for each individual involved.

SMART Goals

Now that we've taken a look at the types of habits that can be the most beneficial to us in our goals, let's take a look at a method for setting goals! The goals that you set should meet five criteria to ensure that your focus is in the most economical and prudent place. Doing so will save you extra effort, and will help you to increase your chances of achieving the goals that you're setting over time.

Let's look at what SMART means!

Specific

Measurable

Attainable

Relevant

Time-based

We'll break this down by letter so you can see precisely what your goals should look like as you're setting them in your day-to-day, and in your long-term planning!

Specific

Having a nebulous goal can make it so much harder to achieve what you want. The more specific you are about the things you want to achieve, the better chance you have of achieving that goal.

You want to state what you'll do, and you want to use action words when you make those statements. For instance, if your whole goal is, "I want to be rich," there aren't a lot of specifics in there and the only verbs in the statement are "want," and "be." Those aren't particularly active words and this statement doesn't really fall into the category of specific.

Now, if you were to say something a little bit more, you could say something like, "I want to develop a new app that will generate $50k in its first year." This is very specific and features words that show action.

Now, once you set this over-arching goal, you can further break down the specifics of that goal. To do this, you can ask yourself some simple questions:

- "What do I want to achieve with this goal?"
- "Where do I want to do this?"

- "What will be my method?"

- "What is my timeline for this goal?"

- "Do I want to work with someone to achieve this? Who?"

- "Are there conditions or limitations with which I should be thinking at this stage?"

- "Why do I want to achieve this goal?"

These questions give you a really great base for understanding your goal, all the intricacies that will come with it, and it gets you into the right frame of mind to begin working on it.

Measurable

Our goals can be hard to quantify when we're in the beginning stages of them. If our ideas are too nebulous, it could be hard to tell if we've even been looking in the right places. Making sure your goal is measurable means taking the time to identify the things that you will see, hear, feel, and sense when you achieve your goal. It means taking the measurable elements of the goal you're setting and working with them.

For this aspect, you will want to gauge quantifiable results. While being happy is a great result for the achievement of a goal, it's hard to quantify. Try looking for something like, "I've gone from needing to walk with a cane, to being able to walk a 5k." These are quantifiable, measurable results that are tangible in nature.

Defining the physical specifications of the goal you're working on achieving is a great way to make it easier to visualize and achieve. You will know when you're on your way!

Attainable

This part of the process can be a little bit hard to swallow. Is the goal that you have in mind attainable? If it isn't, you owe it to yourself to be reasonable and state that it is not currently attainable. This doesn't need to mean that you can't work your way up to it eventually, but if you start to go right for it out of the gate without setting up the preliminary steps, you could be setting yourself up for heartache.

Make sure that, whatever you're shooting for, you're keeping in mind the real-world obstacles that stand between you and that goal!

Relevant

Is this goal something that is relevant to you and what you want for your life? Make sure that you're not setting goals based on the things that others want for your life. Your goals should be your own things that you personally want to accomplish.

Take a look at your motivations behind the goals you have and determine if they're something that is really relevant to you!

Timely

Give yourself a deadline! Remember Parkinson's Law! The time allotted for a task will inevitably be taken up by the things that are needed to complete it.

Put together a flexible timeline for your goal and all the tasks that will be relevant to that goal. Make sure that you make adjustments as you learn about how long things really take, and as you find out more things about your personal capabilities.

Keeping your timeline realistic can do wonders for your morale and it can help you to push harder to achieve the things that you want to achieve in your life. Being too tight with your timelines can set you up for a loss, and that wouldn't be fair either. Being too lenient on your timelines robs you of time that could be allotted for other, more involves tasks on the timeline.

Be sure you're being wise with your time and you will achieve your goals precisely when you mean to.

Setting Your SMART Goals

Be sure that when you're putting your goals together, you're focusing on the positive. If your goal is, "stop smoking," your attention will focus more on the smoking and on the negative.

Base your goal in the positive and you will find that it will bring more positive with it, and your focus will be on a healthier aspect of that goal. For instance, you could be working toward, "six months of nicotine-free living!"

Your focus is on being free of nicotine, on living, and on a precise timeline! Just like with the method of pulling yourself out of procrastination, you give yourself a short timeline. At the end of that timeline, you can reevaluate and keep the train rolling!

Chapter 19 Managing Stress: Tips and Exercises to Reduce Stress

Stepping outside of your comfort zone and developing habits that push you towards your goals naturally come with some side effects, one of which is stress. We try to avoid stress like the plague, and that's partly because we understand more about the effects chronic stress can have on our bodies and mental health. However, not all stress is bad, and part of acquiring mental toughness is learning whether stress is helpful or harmful.

Nevertheless, before we get into that, we're going to look at what the stress response is and why it can be so detrimental.

The definition of stress when the term was coined stated it is "the non-specific response of the body to any demand for change" (Selye, 1936). These responses can be mental, emotional, or physical. Think about all the things your mind and body do when you feel stressed. Your stomach may twist up in knots, anxiety begins to build, and all you can think about is whatever it is that's causing the stress. All of these (and more symptoms) culminate to form what we know to be the stress response. Once it gets going, it's very hard to return to a pre-stress state unless the stressor itself is gone.

There are three different types of stress, according to the American Psychological Association (n.d.).

Acute Stress

The most common and frequently experienced type of stress, acute stress is brief and results from your response to a situation. For example, if one of your kids is sick and there's no one to stay home to take care of them, you may feel tense and irritable, which are both symptoms of acute stress. This type dissipates fairly quickly and goes away entirely once the stressor has been removed or dealt with.

Episodic Acute Stress

This is the next level of acute stress, and you may have guessed by the name that it describes acute stress that happens regularly. If you frequently have tight deadlines at work, you may experience episodes of acute stress whenever the deadline is approaching that then go away once you've handed in your project.

However, this type of stress can also arise, no thanks to your mindset. If you worry a lot or are a perfectionist, you'll experience episodic acute stress. This may lead to stomach problems and emotional distress.

Chronic Stress

Chronic stress is the new buzzword in health and psychology circles. The more our world evolves, the more stressors we're exposed to and, consequently, the more often we feel stressed. Any situation that is not fleeting or easily solved can lead to chronic stress because the stressor never goes away. This can lead to chronic illnesses — aside from stress — that significantly impact your quality of life and shorten your lifespan.

Tips and Exercises to Reduce Stress

Knowing the difference between good and bad stress means nothing if you continue to let the latter beat you up. Instead of allowing yourself to fall apart whenever you feel stress kicking in, turn to these tips so you can acknowledge it without letting it take over.

Accept a Lack of Control

One of the biggest reasons why we feel stressed is that we can't accept that we aren't always in control. We have an obsession with micromanaging because we think that's how we will achieve success. In reality, this tendency to seek control in every situation makes us too rigid and unable to see alternative pathways. Then, when we run into a roadblock, stress comes crashing down because our perceived control has been thwarted.

The key to reducing stress is acknowledging that you're not in control. Instead of letting that idea scare you, let it relieve you of the burden. You're not in control, and that's okay. You don't have to manage your entire life, and that's a good thing. Once you step back and let life happen on its own, you can adjust better when situations change and make decisions from a place of logic instead of fear.

Reduce the Stressors You CAN Control

While most aspects of life are not under your control, there are some things that you can influence. Wherever possible, reduce stress by eliminating your burden and learning to manage tasks better. If you have too much to do at work and it's causing you anxiety, learn to delegate. If you can make a change that will reduce the amount of stress in your life without sacrificing your goals, do it.

Breathe

One of our physical reactions to stress is tension in the jaw, neck, and torso, which can affect our breathing patterns. When our body is deprived of oxygen, it's not happy and will tend to let us know. Combat both the physical and mental reactions by remembering to breathe and employing a breathing exercise when you feel overwhelmed. Counting backwards from 100 while slowly breathing in for one number and out for the next refocuses your brain and takes you out of the situation momentarily.

Leave Room for Fun

Life is supposed to be enjoyable. Whenever possible, leave behind the worry, stress, anxiety, pressure, and seriousness and just let yourself have fun. Go to the park and watch the kids play, take a dip in a lake, or put on your absolute favorite movie and pay attention to every scene and line of dialogue. When we let stress take away our ability to enjoy ourselves, we're at the beginning of the end. No matter how bad things get, you're still alive, so let yourself appreciate that.

Avoid Vices

You may be tempted to turn to cigarettes, alcohol, or drugs when under a lot of stress—don't. No matter how good you may feel after indulging, the underlying issue doesn't go away. Once you sober up, you'll be right back where you started only with a massive headache and a higher risk for lung cancer.

These vices also go against the tenets of mental toughness. Learning to be strong enough to face your issues head on will serve you well in all aspects of life, whether they're stressful or not.

Take Care of Yourself

You can't take care of your life if you don't take care of yourself first. A healthy body and mind are better equipped to deal with life's challenges, so don't neglect either. If you sit on the couch eating junk food all the time, neither your body nor your mind will be in optimal states. The moment a stressor occurs, you'll be knocked down.

Physical and mental strength (and toughness) start on the inside, so once you've built a firm foundation of wellness within yourself, stress from external sources will have a harder time breaking through and getting to you.

Eat well — whatever that means for you. Diet fads come and go, but truly healthy foods never change, so stick to the basics. Get up and move during the day, especially if you feel stress coming on. Do whatever you need to do to prioritize your health because you have nothing without it.

Know When to Ask for Help

You don't have to go through your entire life doing everything by yourself. That's not always a sign of strength. If you try to push through without asking for help, even when you really need it, that's foolhardier than anything. Know when you need help and don't be afraid to get it. Sometimes the stress in our lives is avoidable if we would only take the proper steps to better manage our time and resources. This goes along with reducing the stressors that you can control. Don't let your need to be a tower of strength be the cause of your collapse.

Beyond these tips, just remember that stress is psychological. It all starts in your mind. If you can learn to control your mind through mental toughness, you'll be able to address the root of the problem. Turn your mindset around so that you can turn your life around.

Chapter 20 What Is Emotional Intelligence?

Emotional intelligence is the ability to recognize and understand your own emotions as well as the emotions of others. It has a variety of different definitions with no one definition being superior to the others. Some texts define emotional intelligence as having four fundamental parts which include: managing emotions, perceiving emotions, understanding emotions, and using emotions. Other texts consider emotional intelligence to be self-awareness, social awareness, relationship management, self-management, and emotional intelligence. Still more consider emotional intelligence to be composed of five parts; these five parts are social skills, self-awareness, self-regulation, motivation, and empathy. One thing that is agreed upon is that emotional intelligence consists of being both aware of your own self and your emotions as well as being conscious of the people around you and their emotions.

Emotional intelligence gives you the ability to differentiate between different emotions that you may experience and identify and label each one correctly. This skill is a very important skill for people to possess because understanding your own emotions and being able to differentiate between them gives you the opportunity to control your emotions and take steps to adjust them. For instance, if you notice that a given thing makes you depressed, you can take steps to counter that in advance to avoid or minimize this emotional response.

Understanding and being able to differentiate between the emotions, responses, and behaviors of others allows you to interact better with other people. This is very important because a great deal of our lives has to do with interaction with other people. You can benefit from this in almost every facet of your life. A salesman can understand body language, and facial expressions, and understands which statements a person may take offense.

The Ability to Listen to Your Emotions

Emotional intelligence is also the ability to listen to and adjust your thinking and behavior based on the information that your emotions are giving you.

For it to be a good idea, however, for you to listen to your emotions and be guided by them, you need to have the ability to keep your emotions in balance.

Your emotions need to be under control before it is okay to listen to them. It would not be wise for an overly emotional person to listen to and be guided by his or her emotions. Thus, you must be able first to identify your emotions, and then understand where your emotions are coming from and what triggers them. Is it an event from the past? Is it negative thoughts about your worthiness? Is it an overly inflated ego? It is important to understand whether your emotions are coming from the event or person that you are dealing with or something else before you judge your reaction.

Your emotions need to provide you with accurate information in order for you to be able to use them in a manner that is beneficial to you. Thus, you need to be in tune with your emotions and tune them up from time to time so that the information that they are presenting to you is useful and accurate and thus a good guide for your behavior.

Why Do You Need Emotional Intelligence?

Everyone needs to have emotional intelligence, and it can definitely make your life easier if you have a great deal of emotional intelligence. The ability to understand the way that others are thinking, feeling and may react as well as being in touch with your own emotions that are formed for the situations that are in can help you navigate through situations in daily life far more effectively and with greater ease than you would if you lacked this skill.

It is important for a person to understand how his or her emotions connect to his or her behavior. Emotions have a significant effect on how a person perceives things, and in turn how he or she reacts to it. If you do not understand and are not in control of your emotions, you may not understand the reason for your reaction. Many people never even bother to think about why they react a certain way to certain things. Your behavior directly relates to your reaction to certain stimuli.

Furthermore, the way in which other people react and behave toward you is directly correlated to the emotions that they feel when they are around you as well. So, it is best to be in tune to the so that you can do well. In fact, people with a high degree of emotional intelligence often manipulate other people's emotions to tilt situations in their favor.

When Do You Need Emotional Intelligence?

There are a significant number of situations in life when you need to have emotional intelligence so it would be wise to think that it is always good to have and utilize emotional intelligence. In fact, it can be argued that the only time that you do not need to have emotional intelligence is when you are sleeping...alone. This is because life is filled with interactions between other people and these interactions often involve emotions.

In Relationships

One of the most obvious times in which you can benefit from having emotional intelligence is in your personal relationships. Relationships are often filled with and even based on emotions.

Knowing when your spouse or significant other is happy, upset, or annoyed can help your relationship run a lot smoother, so does knowing the right thing to say and when to say it. Awkward people, people without adequate people skills often have a difficult time meeting people and thus forming relationships. If you have no clue what to say to the opposite sex, when or what they may find offensive, you may have a difficult time finding a mate, most cases are not this extreme, and most people do have some emotional intelligence; however, improving your emotional intelligence can help you to enjoy your relationships more, form more relationships and closer bonds with other people, feel less intimidated in social situations and network better with others.

At Work

Although it may not seem as though emotional intelligence comes into play as much at work, if there are other people around you at work, and these people are likely to experience emotions, then emotional intelligence can be a great asset to you in the workplace. In fact, emotional intelligence can help your workday go more smoothly, help you to get along with your coworkers better, get the people around you to look more favorably upon your ability to do your work and even get you a raise or a promotion that you have wanted for a long time.

The first time you use emotional intelligence at work is at the job interview itself. Since the interviewer may be seeing a number of different candidates, you do not only want to make sure that you impress him or her with your credentials and impressive resume, you also want to make sure that you do not rub the person the wrong way. Yes, catering to your interviewer's emotions is important if you want to land that job.

You know you need to be able to read signals and take hints in order to secure the position. But what does taking hints involve? Taking hints and reading signals involves identifying the emotions of the interviewer and acting according to what is pleasing to him or her. Or, it may mean realizing that this is not a person that you want to work with and that you need to look for another job. Either way, it is important for you to be in tune with the thoughts and feelings of the interviewer so that you can perform well or make a judgement call as to whether this is an environment that you can work in.

Chapter 21 Improve Your Emotional Intelligence Strategies

Your emotional intelligence has absolutely nothing to do with how many books learning you have achieved in life. You can have extensive college degrees and be completely unintelligent with your emotional states, response, and triggers. Complete understanding and mastery of your emotions will place you at the top of the class when it comes to mental toughness.

Understanding Emotional Controls

What is it about emotions that can hang us up when trying to cruise along in life? A major life-altering event is understandable, but what accounts for the brakes being slammed on life with emotions like depression, overwhelming sadness, jealousy, or rage? Are you doomed to being subjected to your daily ration of emotional energy? You can learn to adapt and work around emotions once you have a full understanding of what they are, where they come from, and how much control you can exercise.

What causes an emotional response?

Negative emotions are typically tied to some of our deepest held beliefs about self-worth, life-satisfaction, and abandonment. Positive emotions tend to tie into already held memories of happiness, bliss, acceptance, and affection for others. As social creatures, humans are driven hard by emotions and emotional response to outside stimuli. Although many people define themselves as "loners" or solitary personalities, they are just as socially dependent on feeling confirmation and acceptance as anyone else. It is a part of human nature.

If you get devastating news, such as a death in the family or a serious medical diagnosis, the brain takes in this information, and the electrical activity hits full-tilt. Feeling of impending abandonment and not being able to see the person you love anymore can be temporarily overwhelming. Fear of death can also be a debilitating sensation, initially. The body responds by crashing in a way that causes overwhelming sadness and grief to take over. Getting news of a promotion at work or a new baby on the way can have the opposite effect. It can leave you feeling like you are walking on the clouds. It directly correlates to our deepest held beliefs of self or self-worth and can be a strong response.

How to temporarily push emotions out of the picture

Receiving traumatic news of family illness, accident, or death cannot be completely pushed aside and should not be. It is moments like these that will consume your immediate thoughts and time with good reason. Other, lesser events such as losing your job or a breakup with a partner can be temporarily pushed off when you are trying to make it through a day at work or other activity. A few things to try are:

- Put in earbuds and listen to some uplifting, up-tempo music.

- Send your resume to ten awesome companies offering totally amazing jobs.

- Take yourself out to lunch to a nice, brightly lit café.

- Take a walk and reconnect with nature to regain a calm feeling.

- Avoid talking to others about the issue while emotions are raw.

Identifying Emotional Triggers

Knowing what triggers certain emotions in you is one way to have the information you need to try and avoid situations that can become unpleasant. No one knows and understands your emotional makeup more than you and those closest to you. Unfortunately, you are one of the few that cares about your personal emotional health and well-being. Find out and obey your personal limits on triggering events, information, and subjecting yourself to situations that bring a negative emotional response. Pre-planning is often necessary.

Sad and upsetting events

Hearing news that is upsetting or creates a lingering sadness has a way of completely disrupting your day. It never fails that someone gets upset about an opinion and it can ruin a perfectly good evening. Developing mental toughness should include disciplining yourself to withstand or avoid situations that can lead to triggering feelings of sadness or upset.

The best way to handle emotional triggers is to incorporate avoidance techniques. A few practical ways are:

- Bow out of conversations that are venturing into areas that trigger your emotional response.

- Do not watch the news if the news is upsetting to you.

- Keep conversations light with people you find irritating.

- Change the subject if someone is trying to trigger a response.

- Get your mind off it with the promise you can revisit it at a better time.

- If all else fails, walk away from a triggering event or conversation.

You may have to give these methods a try or come up with a few avoidance techniques of your own. At some point, you will be able to withstand things that used to trigger you as you develop more mental toughness.

Giving and receiving anger

Anger is one emotion that needs to be completely brought under tight control. It is the one that can lead to violent actions brought to you or done by you to others. Rage can get out of control quickly and often with little reason. People have submitted reasons for murder being something as slight as getting an ugly look or being in a bad mood. Trivial reasons for such dastardly crimes are rare, but it happens. It demonstrates how quickly triggering anger can lead to an action that cannot be taken back. It is a lack of self-control that is the polar-opposite of mental strength and toughness.

Before lodging any complaints about the anger dished out to you daily, ask yourself if you are completely innocent of gifting people with an angry tirade now and again. Anger can manifest in many ways, even as passive-aggressive. A few ways we display anger are:

- "Flipping the bird" when someone cuts you off in traffic

- Giving someone the cold shoulder

- Yelling at someone for making a simple mistake

- Mumbling or cursing under your breath when you feel someone is taking too long at the check-out line

- Refusing to hold the elevator or door for someone that you have had a beef within the past

Managing Negative Emotions

Any emotion you experience that interferes with what you are trying to accomplish can be considered negative. You may be besieged with joy that makes it difficult to be still. It is not a wonderful feeling at midnight when you need to be up early for work the next day. Anger, jealousy, insecurity, and any number of emotions that leave you feeling somewhat out of control are negative and need dealt with to experience peace and push towards mental toughness. Never let emotions make you feel tied down and controlled.

When experiencing a negative emotion, ask yourself the following questions:

- Where is the emotion coming from?

- Is it a situation or event you have any control over?

- Will it pass quickly?

- Do you need to change locations or activities for a few minutes or hours?

- Is there something you can do at the moment that will quickly change your state of emotions?

- Is there a pattern in the appearance, such as date, time of day, activity, or people?

- Is the negative emotion coming from you or transferring from someone else?

- Have you done anything in the past that has helped get rid of similar negative emotions?

Combating sadness and depression

Overwhelming feelings of sadness and depression must be eliminated to consider yourself mentally tough. No matter how much you prepare yourself, things will happen that leave hurt, pain, and sadness. The death of a spouse, loss of a pet, a divorce, foreclosure, and many other life events can leave you feeling nothing short of shaken and sad. The danger of not dealing with sadness is that it can lead to depression long-term. A few ways to kick depression to the curb are:

- Give yourself a healthy time limit to begin getting out of the dumps.

- Begin a regular exercise routine and get plenty of sleep.

- Go see a friend and talk.

- Begin seeing a therapist if you have no one to talk to.

- See the doctor to make sure that there are no health problems behind the depression.

- Begin a hobby you find interesting.

- Do plenty of outdoor activities.

- Make sure your home has plenty of natural lighting.

- Avoid alcohol and drugs.

- Do not watch too much television or sit for long periods of time.

- Listen to soothing or uplifting music.

- Take a long shower or bubble bath.

- Get a professional massage.

Pull the fuse on anger

Anger is the single most self-destructive negative emotion. It is imperative that you practice the best anger management techniques possible to pull the fuse if anger is a huge problem for you. One of the best ways to stop yourself in your tracks with anger is to look at a few videos of adults that throw public tantrums. Seeing the cringe-worthy actions and response from those around offers incentive to change your ways.

Always ask yourself why you are feeling so angry. What will it take to make the anger fade at that moment? How is your anger being received? Is there a better way to handle the situation?

Balanced Emotional Health

Finding a healthy balance to your emotions is the preferable way for all people to live. Being too up or too down can be a miserable experience. Learning how to get and keep your emotions in balance is the perfect way to become stronger mentally. You will feel freer to make the decisions you need to and feel less derailed in all you do. Step off the roller coaster ride of emotional turmoil and experience a calmer, less chaotic daily routine. You will wonder how you ever made any progress this long living in an emotional swamp.

Rolling with the punches

Acceptance, in some small measure, is another important part of developing greater control over your emotions and being mentally tough. Days will come that are filled with difficult events, information, and people. Flexibility in your schedule is helpful for the moments you switch to another activity, choose a different store to shop in, or spend time with loved ones. It is difficult to allow things to roll off your back if you are rigid in your demands and time. Develop the best methods of tolerance or avoidance you can use that work for your situation and lifestyle.

Developing and using a sense of humor is another great way to keep rolling when everything around you is going crazy. It is impossible to change the behavior of others, but you can make a point by placing a well-intentioned touch of humor that accentuates the ridiculous displays of unreasonable anger or unreasonable upset you are witnessing. It can stop the activity immediately. It could draw more anger if the person is way out there, so use your better judgment before attempting the humor route. You do not want to end up making the situation worse. If nothing else, you can walk into another area and have a laugh in private.

Refusing to be ruled by emotions

Mental toughness means drawing a line on being ruled and drug around by your emotions or the emotional demonstrations of others. It is not difficult to completely lose control of your life by allowing emotional states to determine what you get done, where you go, and how limited your attempts to accomplish tasks will be. You will never be able to live life to your fullest potential until you have firm emotional control. How controlled are you by emotions? The following list is enlightening:

- You lose at least a half day of work one or two days each week due to personal emotional upheaval.

- Emotional arguments are a near daily occurrence in your home.

- Work stoppage from anger or arguing amongst employees is a frequent problem.

- You have given up on getting along with some people.

- People easily get under your skin.

- You feel tired and depressed daily.

- You feel angry constantly.

- You feel low energy and tired all the time.

- You worry and fret over the smallest details.

- You feel awkward in a group.

- You take statements too personally.

If any of these are a frequent problem, it might be time to begin working on getting better emotional control in your life.

Chapter 22 Traits of Mental Toughness

The unbeatable mind is strong and tough. It is resilient and relentless. It is determined, and it has the willpower and the drive to succeed. We all want an unbeatable mind and often get frustrated when we fall short of what we wanted to accomplish because we just could not stay focused and determined. Focus and determination are both products of having mental strength. These are some of the traits that the unbeatable mind people possess.

There are certain traits or characteristics that a person must possess in order to develop and establish mental toughness. Some of these traits are some important that if you do not possess them, you may need to take the time to develop these traits before you can hope to gain mental toughness.

Traits of the Unbeatable Mind

1) Mental Competency
2) Emotional Intelligence

3) Resilience
4) Willpower
5) A Winner's Mind
6) The Ability to Focus
7) They Surround Themselves with Other People Who Are Mentally Tough
8) They Avoid Trying Too Hard to Go Against the Grain
9) Expect Delayed Gratification

Trait 1: Mental Competency

The first trait that you must possess to develop and sustain a certain level of mental toughness is mental competency. Having a sound and competent mind is the very first thing that you need to gain mental toughness. Mental competency is the ability to make sound judgement decisions. Thus, it is important to pay attention to and take care of your mental health before developing your mental competence. Taking care of your mental health is important to having the proper foundational environment for mental toughness to develop. Disorders such as bipolar disorder can cloud your judgement and make it very difficult for you to develop mental toughness.

Don't assume that your mental health and mental competency does not change when certain things in your life change. If you experience something such as a death or a severe emotional loss or you are going through post-partum depression, or you just entered menopause, take the time to go get your mental health checked out. This is a very important step to developing an unbeatable mind.

Trait 2: Emotional Intelligence

Emotional intelligence can be characterized as a type of emotional competency, similar to mental competency for the emotions. Emotional competency is the ability to identify, understand and control your own emotions while being able to identify and understand the emotions of others and adjust properly to these emotions.

Having a low level of emotional intelligence can make it very hard to succeed in areas of life that involve other people. For instance, a person who lacks emotional intelligence may find it hard to succeed in relationships due to the fact that he cannot identify and understand the emotions of potential dates and mates. This may lead to a significant amount of communication issues, a lack of enjoyment in the relationship, and the inability to form relationships altogether.

Moreover, having a low level of self-awareness can cause you to identify your own emotions improperly. You may fail to realize how you truly feel about a person, job, or issue because you were not in touch with your emotions. This can lead to less satisfaction in these areas of your life. A high level of emotional intelligence leads to self-awareness. A person who has mastered emotional intelligence skills is more likely to do things that lead to a higher level of satisfaction for him or her because he or she knows himself better.

People who excel in the area of emotional intelligence, however, may find it very easy to deal with people and gravitate toward people. The reason that these people tend to gravitate toward other people is that people have a tendency to reach to them well. There are two key factors which have a significant impact on the way in which people react to them, and these are 1) empathy and 2) and increased ability to communicate with others.

Empathy is the ability to understand the thoughts and feelings of another person. It is the ability to put yourself in their shoes so to speak. People who can empathize with others are more likely to make other people comfortable around them and feel relaxed. Furthermore, people tend to feel that the empathetic person cares more about their day or how they are doing than people who have not developed the skill to emphasize with others. This can lead to deeper connections. Thus, a person who has emotional intelligence and can emphasize with others is more like to have more positive strong connections with people than a person who does not know how to emphasize with others. And these strong connections are a support system upon which a person can build more mental toughness.

A person with emotional intelligence has better communication skills. Being able to understand other people's emotions and adjust accordingly aids in conversation skills tremendously. Understanding the emotions of others can keep you from saying things which are off-putting or offensive, both thing that can quickly end a conversation and convince the other person not to communicate as much with you in the future.

Communication skills are derived from not only having the ability to understand emotions and speech; it includes reading and understanding the use of body language, personalities and more. Much of communication is about listening. To be a good listener, you should learn to listen actively. Do not just stand there passively as a conversation is taking place, that a strong interest in the words that are being said. And be sure that you notice the facial expression and the body language. Hand gestures are also good for you to notice. Take in the whole scene and make a judgement with that in mind.

Trait 3: Resilience

Resilience is the cornerstone trait of mental toughness. In fact, many people consider resilience to be the definition of mental toughness. Resilience is the ability to persevere and persist even though the challenges that life brings you. It is the ability to dust yourself off after a setback and get back up and try again and again until you succeed. Resilience is what helps people to overcome the challenges and obstacles that they find when they start trying to achieve a certain goal.

There are a number of factors that make up resilience. One of the factors that play a role in resilience is possessing confidence in yourself. You must have confidence in order to succeed. Confidence is the belief that you can accomplish the goal that you have set out to accomplish, that you are good enough, and you deserve to achieve your goal. To achieve a lofty goal, you have to believe that you can.

Therefore, confidence is also the ability to limit and control your negative beliefs in yourself so that they do not outweigh the positive ones that are telling you that you can succeed. Throughout life, many people have formed a significant amount of negative beliefs about whether or not they can be something that they want to be or do something that they want to do. People may have been led to believe that they are limited by where they are from, how much money they have, their skin color, their looks and more. These beliefs tend to reside in the back of people's minds and stop them from believing that they can achieve certain goals in life and that they need to 'stay in their place' and dream they type of dreams that were made for someone like them.

Peers, teachers, classmates and more may have discouraged a person from trying to achieve certain goals instead of encouraging the person to go after them. Therefore, resilience is the ability to get past these negative affirmations that have been placed in our minds, sometimes over the span of years, and to reprogram ourselves to see our chances of achieving these goals in a more positive manner.

Trait 4: Willpower

People who are mentally tough have a significant amount of willpower. Willpower is the determination that is needed to do things such as lose 50 pounds, stop smoking, stick to an exercise routine and many other things in life.

Willpower is the ability to not give in to your negative desires. It is the ability to resist temptation in order to make changes in your life that will improve your life from its current state. In fact, a survey conducted by the American Psychological Association, it was found that the number 1 barrier that most people cited to making positive changes in their lives was the lack of willpower. Therefore, the most limiting factor that people face, according to the American Psychological

Association is not the lack of money, lack of education, or the lack of time, it is the lack of the ability to resist negative temptation.

Willpower or lack thereof is one of the biggest hurdles that most people face. In order to quit smoking, you need to be able to withstand the urge to do so; but, the majority of people who try to quit smoking fail because their desire to quit is not as strong as their desire to smoke one more cigarette. Even though smokers who want to quit may be aware of all of the negative effects that smoking can have has on them such as a wide variety of health problems, high cost, stained teeth, walls and more, people still lack the sheer determination to quit the habit. A person who has mental toughness, however, is able to channel this determination and use it to effectively quit smoking. And willpower is the key to success in most of the goals that you have in life.

Trait 5: A Winner's Mind

Mentally tough people have the right mindset to achieve the task that they set out to achieve. They believe that they can do it and have a positive attitude and the likelihood that they will succeed. Having a winner's mind is about having the drive to push forward and not allowing yourself to take no for an answer. People with a winner's mind do have the willpower that is necessary to achieve the goals and dreams; in fact, this is something that many people with a winner's mind never even bother to call into question, unlike the rest of us.

Certain aspects are present within the winner's mind. A winner's mind is grateful for the things that he or she has. Being thankful for the things that you have allows you to have a positive attitude despite the things that you lack. A winner is glad for the everyday things that he or she was blessed with that will allow him or her to achieve his or her goals in life.

A winner's mind thinks positive thoughts. There are many people who allow their minds to be clogged with negative thoughts. This is something that is detrimental to their spirit, their mindset, and their likelihood of achieving the goals that they set out to accomplish. Winners concentrate on seeing things in a positive manner. In fact, winners try to surround themselves with a positive vibe and group of people altogether so that their mindset is connected to positivity.

In addition, a winner's mind is always ready and open to learn more and enhance the skills that the person possesses. Winners are constantly learning and developing and evolving in order to stay on top of their game.

Winners are always setting new goals. Once you reach one goal in life, a winner would not be satisfied to just sit back and be content that he or she had achieved that particular goal. Winner's tend to set new goals immediately after achieving one goal; the success of fulfilling one the first goal offers encouragement and confidence that the next goal that is set can be achieved as well. Winners also tend to set these goals in progression, or series, one right after the other, knocking them off like a to-do list. This helps to keep you motivated and striving to achieve more and more.

Trait 6: The Ability to Focus

We've all seen people who do not have a strong ability to focus and are easily distracted. In fact, there is a good chance that you are one of these people if you have not taken the time to try to develop your mental toughness. Mental strength improves your concentration. A significant number of exercises that are designed to help you improve your mental strength are focused on concentration.

Many high-performance athletes have tunnel vision when in their athletic performance mode so that they have a total and complete concentration that allows them to excel. This focus is necessary to make split-second decisions on how to deal with other players in order to come out on top. Many people who have never participated in these types of activities do not understand the type of focused zone these athletes get into and may have never honed their skills to get to total focus on the play at hand.

Trait 7: They Surround Themselves with Other People Who Are Mentally Tough

People with mental toughness tend to surround themselves with other people who are mentally tough. You often find that athletes and entertainers of a certain level tend to associate with each other, and you may have assumed that it is because they are celebrities or because they are highly paid. You may not realize that their work ethic may be part of the reason that they gravitate towards each other. Their careers are so demanding that other people may not understand this and may not agree with doing the same amount of work that they are willing to put in. These high-level performers keep each other on their toes and encourage each other.

And these people all possess a high degree of mental toughness which tends to feed off of each other. They can encourage each other to stay strong and work hard. They illustrate what mental toughness is in a given situation; they support each other and more.

It is rare that you see a person who seems to be strong mentally and emotionally closely associated with someone who is significantly weaker in these two categories. This is because, although the stronger one may rub off on and have an effect on the weaker one, the weaker one has an effect on the stronger one as well. The stronger one is being pulled down, and the weaker one is being pulled up toward a common average strength. This is often uncomfortable for both people. It can be frustrating for the stronger person who may often wonder why the weaker one fails to show as much willpower, determination, and drive, and it can be belittling for the weaker person who may experience insults and a condescending attitude from the other. Thus, it is beneficial for both people in associate more closely with someone on their level of mental strength.

This means that if you desire to develop your mental strength, you need to identify and surround yourself with people who possess mental strength as well. And you may have to eliminate or reduce association with some people who may keep you from reaching higher levels of mental strength.

Trait 8: They Avoid Trying Too Hard to Go Against the Grain

No, you should not always try to simply go with the flow and fit in. And the people known for having very high levels of emotional intelligence definitely stand out; however, there is nothing wrong with trying to fit in a little. Constantly trying to buck the system can get tiring and start to become frustrating.

In addition, this can place more stress and mental strain on a person. This takes up space in a person's minds and takes a good deal of his or her time that could have been spent on something else. Furthermore, trying to be different can start to take a toll on you emotionally. When working on improving emotional intelligence which is covered later in this book, you will learn to identify and understand other people's feelings and reactions and how to adjust to gain better responses from others.

Trait 9: Expect Delayed Gratification

People with mental strength do not need to reap immediate benefits for their work and actions. They are fine with the benefits coming in time for the work that they did and the time that they put in. Seeking instant gratification can keep you from achieving what you could have achieved if you understood that the payout for the work that you put in does not always come immediately. Sometimes, it may take years to see the fruits of your labor. It is still important to keep going in order to see the benefits of your work.

Honing your mental strength will allow you to see that rewards are not the only good thing that you receive from your hard labor. There is the pride of a job well done and accomplishing your goals. You can also enjoy helping others in some way. And the rewards for your hard labor will come in time.

Chapter 23 Building Mental Strength

While telling a person to adopt the traits of the mentally strong is a good way to develop mental toughness, it may not always be enough. In a way it's a bit like telling a person that in order to be healthy you need to eat right, exercise, and get plenty of rest. Such advice is good and even correct, however it lacks a certain specificity that can leave a person feeling unsure of exactly what to do. Fortunately, there are several practices that can create a clear plan of how to achieve mental toughness. These practices are like the actual recipes and exercises needed in order to eat right and get plenty of exercise. By adopting these practices into your daily routine, you will begin to develop mental toughness in everything you do and in every environment you find yourself in.

Keep your emotions in check

The most important thing you can do in the quest for developing mental toughness is to keep your emotions in check. People who fail to take control of their emotions allow their emotions to control them. More often than not, this takes the form of people who are driven by rage, fear, or both. Whenever a person allows their emotions to control them, they allow their emotions to control their decisions, words, and actions. However, when you keep your emotions in check, you take control of your decisions, words, and actions, thereby taking control of your life overall.

In order to keep your emotions in check you have to learn to allow your emotions to subside before reacting to a situation. Therefore, instead of speaking when you are angry, or making a decision when you are frustrated, take a few minutes to allow your emotions to settle down. Take a moment to simply sit down, breathe deeply, and allow your energies to restore balance. Only when you feel calm and in control should you make your decision, speak your mind, or take any action.

Practice detachment

Another critical element for mental toughness is what is known as detachment. This is when you remove yourself emotionally from the particular situation that is going on around you. Even if the situation affects you directly, remaining detached is a very positive thing. The biggest benefit of detachment is that it prevents an emotional response to the situation at hand. This is particularly helpful when things are not going according to plan.

Practicing detachment requires a great deal of effort at first. After all, most people are programmed to feel emotionally attached to the events going on around them at any given time. One of the best ways to practice detachment is to tell yourself that the situation isn't permanent. What causes a person to feel fear and frustration when faced with a negative situation is that they feel the situation is permanent. When you realize that even the worst events are temporary, you avoid the negative emotional response they can create.

Another way to become detached is to determine the reason you feel attached to the situation in the first place. In the case that someone is saying or doing something to hurt your feelings understand that their words and actions are a reflection of them, not you. As long as you don't feed into their negativity you won't experience the pain they are trying to cause. This is true for anything you experience. By not feeding a negative situation or event with negative emotions you prevent that situation from connecting to you. This allows you to exist within a negative event without being affected by it.

Accept what is beyond your control

Acceptance is one of the cornerstones of mental toughness. This can take the form of accepting yourself for who you are and accepting others for who they are, but it can also take the form of accepting what is beyond your control. When you learn to accept the things you can't change, you rewrite how your mind reacts to every situation you encounter. The fact of the matter is that the majority of stress and anxiety felt by the average person is the result of not being able to change certain things. Once you learn to accept those things you can't change, you eliminate all of that harmful stress and anxiety permanently.

While accepting what is beyond your control will take a little practice, it is actually quite easy in nature. The trick is to simply ask yourself if you can do anything at all to change the situation at hand. If the answer is 'no,' simply let it go. Rather than wasting time and energy fretting about what you can't control adopt the mantra "It is what it is." This might seem careless at first, but after a while you will realize that it is a true sign of mental strength. By accepting what is beyond your control, you conserve your energy, thoughts, and time for those things you can affect, thereby making your efforts more effective and worthwhile.

Always be prepared

Another way to build mental toughness is to always be prepared. If you allow life to take you from one event to another you will feel lost, uncertain, and unprepared for the experiences you encounter. However, when you take the time to prepare yourself for what lies ahead, you will develop a sense of being in control of your situation at all times. There are two ways to be prepared, and they are equally important for developing mental toughness.

The first way to be prepared is to prepare your mind at the beginning of each and every day. This takes the form of you taking time in the morning to focus your mind on who you are, what you are capable of, and your outlook on life in general. Whether you refer to this time as mediation, contemplation, or daily affirmations, the basic principle is the same. You simply focus your mind on what you believe and the qualities you aspire to. This will keep you grounded in your ideals throughout the day, helping you to make the right choices regardless of what life throws your way.

The second way to always be prepared is to take the time to prepare yourself for the situation at hand. If you have to give a presentation, make sure to give yourself plenty of time to prepare for it. Go over the information you want to present, choose the materials you want to use, and even take the time to make sure you have the exact clothes you want to wear. When you go into a situation fully prepared, you increase your self-confidence, giving you an added edge. Additionally, you will eliminate the stress and anxiety that results from feeling unprepared.

Take the time to embrace success

One of the problems many negatively-minded people experience is that they never take the time to appreciate success when it comes their way. Sometimes they are too afraid of jinxing that success to actually recognize it. Most of the time, however, they are unable to embrace success because their mindset is simply too negative for such a positive action. Mentally strong people, by contrast, always take the time to embrace the successes that come their way. This serves to build their sense of confidence as well as their feeling of satisfaction with how things are going.

Next time you experience a success of any kind, make sure you take a moment to recognize it. You can make an external statement, such as going out for drinks, treating yourself to a nice lunch, or some similar expression of gratitude. Alternatively, you can simply take a quiet moment to reflect on the success and all the effort that went into making it happen. There is no right or wrong way to embrace success, you just need to find a way that works for you. The trick to embracing success is in not letting it go to your head. Rather than praising your efforts or actions, appreciate the fact that things went well. Also, be sure to appreciate those whose help contributed to your success.

Be happy with what you have

Contentment is another element that is critical for mental toughness. In order to develop contentment, you have to learn how to be happy with what you have. This doesn't mean that you eliminate ambition or the desire to achieve greater success, rather it means that you show gratitude for the positives that currently exist.

After all, the only way you will be able to truly appreciate the fulfillment of your dreams is if you can first appreciate your life the way it is.

One example of this is learning to appreciate your job. This is true whether you like your job or not. Even if you hate your job and desperately want to find another one, always take the time to appreciate the fact that you have a job in the first place. The fact is that you could be jobless, which would create all sorts of problems in your life. So, even if you hate your job, learn to appreciate it for what it is. This goes for everything in your life. No matter how good or bad a thing is, always appreciate having it before striving to make a change.

Be happy with who you are

In addition to appreciating what you have you should always be happy with who you are. Again, this doesn't mean that you should settle for who you are and not try to improve your life, rather it means that you should learn to appreciate who you are at every moment. There will always be issues that you want to fix in your life, and things you know you could do better. The problem is that if you focus on the things that are wrong you will always see yourself in a negative light. However, when you learn to appreciate the good parts of your personality, you can pursue self-improvement with a sense of pride, hope, and optimism for who you will become as you begin to fulfill your true potential.

Chapter 24 Rewarding Yourself

Celebrate your successes. Find humor in your failures – Sam Walton

Rewarding yourself from time to time for efforts taken is a good habit to adopt and a key part of the process that shouldn't be overlooked. Why you may wonder?

Because rewarding yourself motivates you and inspires you to continue taking action. By rewarding yourself, your mind will unconsciously start associating good feelings with finishing tasks. In other words, your mind will start relating positive rewards to each effort that you take. Do not allow your ego to run your life. You will find plenty of stories about rich people with deep regrets of not balancing their work with breaks. Work smarter, not harder. I sit back and smile when people declare they are the hardest workers (working 16-20 hours a day for active income), never sleep, and how much they love the grind. "Have fun," I tell them. I'll be the most efficient worker, I set up my businesses to grow while I sleep gaining passive income, and I will enjoy the grind from a place of want, not need. That's a long-term winning mindset.

Successful people reward themselves from time to time so that the effort feels worthwhile. You see it does you no good if you fail to reward yourself because as time goes by you may start getting a feeling of burnout and lack of desire to take action. This is especially true if you had to push yourself harder to take action. Therefore, coming up with a reward system is mandatory if you desire to be successful.

How then do you begin rewarding yourself? Rewarding yourself is fairly straightforward.

Method 1: Go out on a small trip

The first method that you should consider is that of taking yourself out. It doesn't matter how much you love the work you do. If you do it incessantly without taking even a small break, you will eventually burn out.

Going out on a small vacation is a good way to break off and renew your enthusiasm, energy and recharge your batteries . In addition, it helps you put things in focus.

There are lots of places you could go. You could try museums, malls, aquariums, open-air markets, the beach or any other place that is out of your normal routine. A good time to take small vacations like these is during weekdays when people are typically at work. During these times, these places are less crowded.

A key thing to keep in mind though is that you need to keep it short. Somewhere between two to four days is ideal. A short vacation will get rid of the fear that gropes you when you imagine of getting back to a mountain of work.

Method 2: Buying your favorite food

Another great way to reward yourself is treating yourself to your favorite food. When it comes to food, we all have our personal preferences of what we like best. What better way to reward all that discipline to get that work done than to simply go out and buy that food that you've craved for recently.

Thus, go out and grab that ice cream, drink a glass of wine, that pizza, or that cake. You could even cook your favorite meal if you wanted to. It doesn't matter what you prefer, you'll have to decide for yourself on this one. As long as it's something that you don't consume often so that it ends up feeling special to you once you take it.

Method 3: Reward yourself with self-care

Taking care of yourself is another way to reward your hard work and good behavior. We all love ourselves and would like to look and feel good. Making this part of your reward system can be an extremely powerful way to getting things done and becoming more self-disciplined.

There are countless ways of rewarding yourself with self-care. I will highlight a few ways so that you can get the idea and come up with unique ideas of your own. Some good ways of caring for yourself include:

- Going out and getting a manicure/pedicure

- Getting a new tattoo or piercing

- Taking a friend out for a meal and ordering whatever you desire on the menu

- Doing any activity that makes you feel free or similar to a child (e.g., amusement parks, concerts)

- Getting a massage at your favorite parlor

- Watching a great movie

Method 4: Take yourself out for some shopping

Another way that might work and make you feel good about yourself and strive to work better is to go out for some shopping. Although I wouldn't recommend reckless spending that would drive you to debt or make your broke, some of us just want our money to feel better than just numbers in the bank. You may want to compensate for that feeling by buying something.

For this reason, I will recommend one way for getting around the problem of overspending.

I recommend setting up a rewards account. This is like a savings account, only meant for buying rewards for yourself. Periodically, put some money into this account and reserve it for when you accomplish tasks successfully. Then, once you hit a significant milestone, you can dig into your rewards account and take yourself out for some shopping.

This will help you avoid overspending and still allow you to buy things for yourself as a way of making yourself feel good.

Method 5: Treat yourself to something fun but free

While buying yourself things like food, clothes, items and vacations are great ways for rewarding yourself, you don't have to make it all about money. All things considered, I would always advise that you seek ways of rewarding yourself that will involve little to no money. That way, you won't risk your financial freedom or stability. Always finding an excuse to spend money is not a great way to financial prosperity. That being said, here are a number of ways you can reward yourself and not spend money:

- Try going to a nice park/landmark in your town and enjoy nature

- Attend a free social event

- Play a video game at home

- Take a small nap

- Go out and take photos or videos.

As you can see, with a little creativity, you could come up with great ways to have fun but still avoid spending money.

All in all, this chapter has to some degree provided you with great ideas of rewarding yourself. Rewarding yourself is a great and fun part of cultivating self-discipline. Being mentally tough is good and this book has covered a huge part of doing that. However, what is even more important so that the good habits stick is to reward yourself consistently. It provides the much-needed incentive to keep pursuing your goals on your way to success.

Chapter 25 Strategies to be Quiet and Strong in Every Situation

When you are faced by a serious life situation, the first reaction is always to panic not knowing that severe stress and anxiety can cause a complete mental meltdown. As a result, you can end developing long term health damage as well as reduce your ability to perform optimally when required to. Most of the world's top achievers, athletes, artists, and entrepreneurs could not have achieved their heights of success without mastering how to remain calm and collected when under pressure be it work or life-related. As a matter of fact, they have developed and maintain a certain psychological state of readiness and mental preparedness that helps them to accept situations much faster and address them calmly because they understand that situations van change abruptly but they do not define who they are or what the future holds for them. Circumstances and the people around you will often break you down. But if you keep your heart open to receive and give love, the mind focused and continue to move towards the right direction, it will always be easier for you to recover from the break downs and come back as a much stronger and more knowledgeable person. Here are tips on how to remain calm and collected at the height of pressure.

Accept the reality of the situation at hand

Through life, you can't discover peace. Instead of avoiding it, life spins every hour with unexpected modifications and takes every shift and experience as a growth challenge. Either it will offer you what you want, or the next stage will educate you. It does not guarantee any challenges and no hard work or noise before you find peace and good fortune in life. It implies to be in the midst and stay calm in your core. It's about letting your thoughts know how things should be. This isn't simple, of course; it's going to be a continuous fight. It's nevertheless infinitely simpler than fighting to adapt your life to some old delusion. It is also a trip that is endlessly more pleasing. There is peace, beauty and there is happiness when it works if you can separate from ancient beliefs. Honestly, life is too brief for you to go to war. Misappropriate expectations often lead to the greatest disappointments in our life. The first step towards happiness is to let go of unnecessary expectations. Come from a spirit of peace and acceptability and you can cope with and develop beyond virtually anything.

Understand that everything is temporary

Even when the storms are heavy, it eventually stops to rain. You also get a cure whenever you get hurt. Additionally, you are reminded every morning that light always comes after darkness, but choose to think that the night (dark moments in life) will continue forever. That's not going to happen because nothing lasts forever.

So if it's nice, appreciate it right now. It's not ever going to last. Don't care if things are bad, as it will never last. It doesn't just mean you can't laugh because life isn't simple at the time. It does not mean that you can't smile just because you're bothered by something. You get a fresh start and a fresh end at every time. Every second, you get a second opportunity. All you need is do the best you can.

Always push yourself to take another step forward no matter what you are going through

I am confident that about half the difference between good individuals and everybody else is sheer perseverance, this is after studying the lives of many successful individuals. We need to know the beauty of effort, patience, and perseverance in a society that wants fast outcomes. Be powerful, current and unwavering. Usually, the most beautiful smiles are those which have fought through tears. Because failures often ultimately lead to breakthroughs. Each error, heartbreak, and loss has its own answer, a subtle lesson for your performance and result from next time around. So it is you that is the most credible to predict your own future.

Enjoy life today, rather than just looking over it as it passes. Do not allow the few things out of control to interfere with the endless array of things you can control. The reality is that sometimes we all lose. The bigger reality is that we never have a single loss. Learn from your experiences and become wiser. Good things don't finally happen for those who wait: nice things come for those who remain patient as they work hard for what they most want in life, in good times and bad. This is about bravery. It is about being extremely scared and still proceeding to take the next step regardless.

Use positivity and do not let negativity bring you down

There might be no apparent reason today to be positive, but there is no need for a reason. Being always positive is a life strategy and not a response to something nice that might have happened. In fact, the ideal time to overly positive in life is when everything around seems negative and the world seems to be against you in every aspect. It is hard but achievable. Long-term happiness is not lack of issues, but the capacity to address them. Bring your consciousness to your own internal strength and positive position. You are responsible for how you respond in your lives to individuals and activities. You can either offer your life negative energy or choose to be positive by concentrating on the good things that really matter. So speak more about your blessings than today's issues. In other words, don't expect a favorable reason. Choose to be positive about your position, your opportunities and what you can do to get from one point to another. Look for ways to convey your favorable view rather than seeking reasons for being positive. Work to bring this vision to your lives and to enjoy the rewarding results you achieve.

Focus on achieving small fixes

Do not envision mountains in your mind. Don't attempt all at once to conquer the world. You unnecessarily make life difficult and frustrating if you look for instant gratification (large, fast fixes). Instead of making a small, beneficial investment in yourself at every time and the prizes will naturally follow. It's simple to discover a lot of small stuff when all is broken. Even the most important beneficial effort can create a major difference when nothing seems to be correct. Understand those times, when you are faced by the greatest adversity, are times when you encounter the greatest opportunities in life. If issues arise in every direction, it means that there is some great value somewhere waiting to be discovered and created. It's simple to get lulled into an indulgence routine when everything's well. How unbelievably capable and resourceful you maybe is simple to forget. Resolve to continue with small fixes daily. These little tweaks bring you to where you want to be in the long run. Every day, dense and thin, small steps, short leaps, and small fixes (small repetitive modifications) will take you places.

Look for something to appreciate no matter how small it may be

You may not have what you want and you may be very sad, but you can still enjoy more than enough at this time. Do not spoil what you have by wanting what you don't have; remember that what you got now was once just one of your desires. It is a sign of management and strength to remember that being positive in an adverse position is not naive. If you have so much to cry about and complain about, it is okay to mourn, but it is also important to smile and enjoy your life. So don't pray for the great miracles and forget to give thanks for the usual gifts in your life, simple but not that small. It may seem strange to be grateful for those ordinary events in your life, but it is precisely by being grateful that you can turn the ordinary into the uncommon and remain calm amidst pressure. Think of all the beauty around you, see it and smile. It is not gladness that makes us grateful at the end of the day, but gratitude that makes us happy. The most strong happiness activity here is to show gratitude for the excellent stuff you have.

Accord yourself the attention you deserve

It does not serve you to resist and ignore your own emotions and feelings. This leads to stress, disease, confusion, broken friendships, anger, and depression. Anyone who has had any of the above knows that those mental statements are terribly unhealthy and it is nearly impossible to escape them if you have the habit of self-disregard. You must confess to having spent too much of your life attempting to diminish yourself to a certain extent. Trying to be smaller in size, less sensitive, quieter, and less needy, have fewer opinions, and just be less of you simply because you were avoiding to push people away or to make feel like you are too much of a burden. You just wanted to fit in and make people like you by creating a certain good impression. You wanted to be needed.

For years, therefore, in order to please others, you have sacrificed yourself. You've endured for years. But you're tired of the pain and shrinking yourself. Good! It's not your job to make someone else's idea about a valuable human being shift who you are. You're valuable. Not because others believe you are, but because you breathe your own air, so you matter. Your ideas are important. Your emotions are important and your voice counts. And you must be who you are, and live your reality, with or without anybody's approval or authorization. Even if it turns the heads of individuals. Even though it does not make them easy. Even if they decide to quit, refuse to shrink your personality. Choose to give yourself the best in life, pursue your dreams and goals, and spare enough time for yourself. Above all, honor your emotions and feelings because self-care defines you. Once you take care of yourself and focus on being the best you can be, it will be easier for you to deal with people and situation under stressful conditions.

Always remember that everyone suffers and experience pain in life. But it is how people deal with adversities at the height of pressure that defines their level of success. Remaining calm during stressful situations helps you to make rational decisions and tap into your mental strength to ensure that you are not swayed by emotions. The key is to use your past life experiences to grow and move towards your achieve your goals a step at a time. When you remain calm and collected when under pressure you only give yourself the power to come up with the ideal solutions but also get to learn how to deal with future situations like the one you experienced. When you apply what you learn now in future plans, actions, and choices, you move forward and certain challenges also become easy to deal with. This is because, you took advantage of a stressful situation to learn, become stronger and wiser. It is not easy to remain calm under pressure because we are all humans and we are bound to react when our emotions are altered by situations. However, it is achievable and totally worth it in the end. Find what calms you down when stressed or under pressure and use it to remain motivated and positive to carry on with work.

Successful people are mentally tough, to be successful in life, you have to be well prepared mentally, whether it is in your family, business, work or education. You have to have some level of mental development to be able to handle objection, the good and bad side of life.

Mental toughness therefore is very relevant and important to every individual. The world population keeps increasing, so many challenges coming up on daily basis. So, you get uncomfortable sometimes, because everything going around you tends to affect you, from politics, leadership, work, business, family etc. everyone seems to be involved and affected and then some things happen that affects you.

The truth you cannot deny and avoid is the fact that as long as we are all humans, everyone needs mental toughness. When the theory of survival of the fittest was propounded, other theories later emerged which postulates that some living things will have to struggle for their survival and it is those living things that were better adapted to changes in their environment that will be able to survive the changes in their environment. Therefore, you should know by now, that there will always be changes in our life and environment, the question is "how well will you be able to adapt to such changes?"

Secondly, ask yourself "have you developed that features that will enable you to carry out your own adaptation"?

Then it is very clear that one of the distinctive features you will need to develop is your level of mental toughness. Whether you like it or not, you need to develop yourself mentally and it will start somewhere, you may be scared right now on how to begin, let me tell you something, your waiting days are over, the simple truth now is that you have to get things started, taking actions is what you really need, and by the time you start with a single step that you decide to take now, you will sooner or later look back and see the distance you would have covered.

Don't wait any longer, take that bold step in the right direction, follow the basic principles and teachings as explained in this book, step by step and one at a time, always refer back to the contents and read to gain mastery of the various approaches and directives given in order to advance further.

The moment is now; get the right mentality to handle any situation you find yourself no matter what the circumstances. Be mentally tough and you will be victorious forever!

Let's hope it was informative and able to provide you with all of the tools you need to achieve your goals whatever it is that they may be. How amazing it must have been for you to realize that your mind is the primary determinant of where you are in life. It determines how quickly you move or how much you hesitate. Heck, it even determines how healthy you are. For these reasons, you need to ensure that your mind is continually tough to withstand the challenges that come about and to keep yourself moving ahead.

It helps when you work on yourself, using your abilities as a benchmark for future improvements, but you could also get inspiration from the works of great men and women that have achieved success in their lifetimes. See what they did when the odds were against them. See what happened when they listened to other people rather than to their own voices. Use their lives as lessons for your own life. You do not have to go through a lesson yourself to learn; other people make great illustrations too.

Chapter 26 Depression

Depression is a severe common psychological disorder that has an emotional impact on how you think, how you feel, and how you act. In this regard, depression results in an emotional state of sadness and continuous disinterest with activities that someone once liked. Fortunately, this disorder is treatable despite the detrimental effects that it possesses on an individual. In the current society, depression has become one of the significant health concerns that have necessitated governments and institutions to engage in an educative undertaking to inform the public on the prevalence of depressive symptoms among youths and the general populace within any community. It is quite certain that you as an individual, in one way or another, have heard or read the information that pertains to depression, or better still through mainstream media outlets understood discussions that were based on despair and its impact on the community as a whole.

Depressive indications can vary from trivial to severe states that involve having or possessing thoughts about death or suicide, concentration difficulty, loss of productive energy or increased exhaustion, continuous feelings of sadness, trouble sleeping, and feeling worthless among many other indicators. Even though it is apparent that in one instance one can possess some of the symptoms identified above, you should note that for a diagnosis of depression to be passed then these symptoms should last for at least two weeks. This is because, some of the warning signs associated with depression are sometimes encountered or experienced daily; thus, one can rush into the conclusion that they are depressed. Unfortunately, this might not be the case, since for such symptoms to be regarded as signs of depression, they have to last for at least two weeks. As a result, researchers have stated that depression is very much different from sadness or mourning. This is because it is a regular occurrence for feelings of sadness and withdrawal from daily lifestyle to develop as a response to the situation: being sad does not signal that you are depressed. Since such occurrences share similar features to depression, they possess different characteristics and qualities.

Anxiety is very different from depression since it entails fear that is characterized by behavioral disturbances. From this perspective, you can discern that anxiety is an intense, excessive, and continuous fear and worry about daily experiences or situations that are characterized by fast breathing, increased heart rate, and sweating to mention a few. Although there are common causes of anxiety that do not have a significant impact or effect on your life. Some of these common causes include public speaking, taking a test or exam, or going for an interview. Anxiety only becomes problematic when possessing anxious feelings to become consistent and persistent that they start to interfere with your regular life. This brings us to the topic of anxiety disorders, a group of mental illnesses that affect you from carrying on with your daily life. The good news about having such kind of complications is that it is treatable just like depression is.

Having that anxiety disorder can be treated, one recommended approach for managing such a condition that you are likely to encounter is therapy for anxiety disorders or mentioned as anxiety therapy. Anxiety therapy comes out as the best option for treating anxiety when compared to medication.

Chapter 27 Identifying Problem and Negative Thoughts Patterns

Social anxiety comes with harmful and destructive thoughts. You need to be observant so that you do not hurt yourself in the process. The negative thinking is likely to rob you of the confidence that you have and feel that you cannot stand going before people. The thoughts instill fear in you, and you end up avoiding social gatherings. When you subject your opinions to negative thinking always, it will result in negative emotions. It can end up making you feel bad and can even lead to depression. The thoughts that you have will determine your mood for your entire day. Positive thinking will make you happy, and you will have a good feeling. Finding a way to suppress negative thoughts will be of importance to you. Replace them with positive ones so that they will not torment you. Some of the negative thoughts that come along with social anxiety are;

Thinking That People as bad

When you are in a social setting, each person tends to be busy with their issues. You can meet a calm person and begin a friendship if you can build a good rapport. When you have social anxiety, you are likely to avoid people and think that people do not care about you. You may feel that you don't see your importance being there while as you are the one who is avoiding them. When you find yourself in such a situation in a social setting, its time you know that you have to handle your social anxiety. That will make you feel like the people around you do not like you and hate you for no reason.

Unnecessary Worry

It is obvious to have unnecessary worry when you have social anxiety. Even when you are on time, you are always worried that you will get late. You will portray a bad image for getting there late. When in a family setting, you are worried that your partner will scold you for lateness. You do things in a hurry so that you do not get late even when you have enough time to go to your thoughts. When you have someone else to accompany you, you will make them do things in a rush. You think like they are consuming all the time and they will be your reason for being late. You will even, at times, threaten to leave them if they don't do things quicker than they are already doing.

When you are needed to make a presentation, you get worried about whether the audience is going to like it or not. You are not sure whether there is someone else who will do better than you. The worry will make you start thinking that your boss will not like what you have even before they make their remarks. You believe that you have nothing exciting to say. The worry will make you lose strength, and any change you feel makes you think that you are not ready. When you start experiencing such concern, you need to know that you have social anxiety. You require to have an approach that is appropriate to handle your social stress so that it will not escalate into something worse.

Judging Yourself

Judging yourself is the worst thing you will ever go, and that will make you fear. Deciding whether you will find pleas people or not will make you have much social anxiety. You will be nervous when you start thinking about how people are thinking about your physical appearance. Judging how you other people will view you will make your self-esteem go down. The people you are worried about will think you do not look outstanding may not have an interest in how you look but what you have to deliver. At times, people do not pay attention to the minor details that are making you judge yourself unnecessarily.

Criticism

Anytime you know that you will intermingle with people, you fear they will criticize you. You do not even have a valid reason why they will criticize you, but you think it is not wise for you to join them. It is a negative thought, and you need to stop thinking in that direction. No one is going to critic you for no reason, and that should not be considered close to you. You will fear to go to social gatherings, and you will deny yourself an opportunity to learn from your fellow partners. Fearing criticism will make you be an introvert, and this will make you mean that you will miss much when you choose to stay indoors. When you say something, and you get someone to challenge you, it will help you be more creative. Criticism is not evil even though that people with social anxiety do not like a situation where they are subject to critics. They will avoid such situations at all cost for fear of humiliation.

Negative thoughts will only escalate worry as well as fear in you. For you to avoid negative thoughts, you can practice cognitive-behavioral therapy. That will replace your negative thoughts with those that are accurate as well as encouraging. Though it will take quite some time to replace the negative thoughts, practicing healthy thinking daily will make that natural to you. If you have social anxiety and you feel that all the approaches you use are not helpful, seek the help of a therapist. Positive thinking will help you in coping with social anxiety. When you notice that you have negative thoughts disturbing you, you should try to drop that with immediate effect. Filter the bad and focus on the good. To change how you are thinking, the first thing you need to do is try and understand how your thinking pattern is at the moment. Do not view yourself as failure always because that will never change your thinking patterns. When you avoid negative thoughts, you will be in an excellent position to fight social anxiety.

Prejudgment

Although it is wise to think about the future, the art of judging tends to be detrimental. In other words, the aspect of prejudging situations tends to be worse, especially when the opposite of the expectations is meant. In most cases, social anxiety disorder tends to cause people to decide the results of a particular situation. It is worth noting that prejudgment is done in regards to the history or rather a forecast of what might happen in the future.

In most cases, the people who are involved in this practice are always negative. Thus, they will think evil of someone and need up piling unnecessary pressure on someone. There are cases where the prejudgment causes one to overthink rather than spend quality time improving on their lives. In other words, prejudgment may force one to change all her aspects in an attempt of meeting the expectations of the peers. The peers will, in most cases, demand or look for everyday things. However, there are cases where the prejudgment predicts a near future that is yet to be accomplished. The aspect causes one to fear as they loom for an alternative as well as ways of meeting the expectations. However, when the expectations aren't satisfied, the anxiety of what the society will say pile up, and one may quickly lose the focus.

Blame Transfer

When a society or the peers piles up unnecessary pressure on someone, the chances of missing the mark is quite easy. In other words, one quickly loses focus and misses the point. As a means of evading the shame or rather the punishment, the victims, in most cases, transfer the blame. For instance, if it issues to deal with academics, the victim may start claiming that time wasn't enough to deliberate on all issues. Others may associate their failures with the climatic changes or the lack of favorable conditions for working. There are cases where the victims tend to be genuine and claim diseases as the cause of their failure. However, the art of transferring blames from one point to another tends to be detrimental and shows signs of being irresponsible.

Procrastination

One of the significant effects of social anxiety is that is causes one to fail in deliberating on duties and transfer them to a later day. In other words, procrastination becomes the order of the day. However, it is worth noting that with procrastination, the expectations are never met. The fear, as well as the sensation of being anxious sets in. In other words, the victim starts feeling as if they are a failure in the collective and loses focus.

More time is wasted as they try to recollect themselves up. More fear sets in and the victim may end up being restless. Improper management of time is the primary cause of procrastination. In other words, the lack of planning causes individuals to keep working over the same issues and forget about others. For instance, scholars may spend more time with the subjects they like and forget about the others. In other words, they may end up forgetting that all the items will be examined in the long run. The sensations bring more fear and restless.

In most cases, the realization that all the aspects will be tested in the long run causes most of the scholars to be anxious about the result. In most cases, the tensing moment tends to escalate when there is no time left to deliberate on all issues. The fear of failure then worsens the situation. In most cases, when the scholars realize that they haven't done all that is supposed to be done, the feeling of loss of hope and expectations of failure sets in. They start figuring about the failure they are about to experience. In other words, they start thinking of what society expects from them. The feeling of anxiety sets in, and they may not be able to deliberate on issues effectively.

Social anxiety may affect the way people lead their lives. In other words, the perception or rather the sensations that people have over someone tend to change the way one relates to society. For instance, if society expects excellence in terms of academics from you, you have to work hard and meet all their expectations. In such cases, there is a sensation of fear or rather the feeling of anxiety that sets in. One starts to fear what society will judge their actions or results.

In most cases, the victim becomes restless and quickly loses focus over issues at hand. They may start desiring to meet the expectations of their peers as well as the rest of society and in the long run, lose their purpose. The aspect creates some sense of irresponsibility that acts as a significant cause of failure and total loss when one is having extreme anxiety over anything.

Our thoughts are interconnected with our feelings and behaviors. The way we think affects both how we feel and act. The first step toward recovering from negativity is identifying various negative thinking patterns. When you take note of your negative thoughts, you get a better understanding of your mind and emotions and are in a much better position to develop positive thoughts.

Some types of negative thoughts include, I'm so stupid, I'm so foolish, and, I'm unlucky.

If you find it difficult to be introspective and admit to your negative thoughts, you should ask a trusted friend or family member to keep track of your negative ways of thought.

Find Out the Causes of Your Negative Thought Patterns

The next challenge is to identify the sources of your negative thoughts. For instance, if one of your negative thoughts is, I'm ugly, no one likes me! try to understand the action or event that triggered this thought. Being good at identifying the causes of our negative thoughts calls us to be introspective. Maybe the source of your negative thought is your childhood abuse. If a close family member told you that you are not beautiful, you might have taken it to heart, and have been since looking for evidence to support your flawed belief. A member of the opposite sex might look at you with a frown – for other reasons of course – but you will still deduct from their facial expression that they find you ugly.

Highlight Unhelpful Thought Patterns

It is one thing having negative thought patterns, and it is another having unhelpful thought patterns. These are also known as core beliefs. The unhelpful thought patterns are ingrained into a person's psyche. Unhelpful thought patterns tend to be divorced from reality. For instance, if you have been telling yourself, "I'm stupid," for long enough, it will cease being just a negative thought and graduate into a core belief. This will lead you to automatically shunning opportunities and people that you consider too smart for you.

List down the Consequences of Your Negative Thoughts

To be more involved in actively changing your negative thought patterns, you have to identify the consequences that you suffer. For instance, if your negative thought, I'm foolish causes you to detach yourself from your peers or stops you from going for the opportunities that you deserve, take note of these consequences so that you may increase your resolve to change your situation. At one point, you will have had enough and decide that you want to change. You may also list down past negative experiences and consequences that occurred as a result of negative thinking patterns.

Keep a Record of Your Thoughts

Using a worksheet, track the number of negative thoughts that you experience on a daily or weekly basis. Also, note down the ideas that support a thought and the ideas that do not support a thought. For instance, if one of your negative thoughts is, I'm a loser, ideas that do not support this negative thought include, "I'm a great person", "I have a sharp mind", and "I don't need everyone to like me!" Try to determine the days during which you experience low cases of negative thought patterns and the days when the negativity shoots through the roof.

Avoid Negative Language

Create a list of negative words that you use often. For instance, "can't" and "won't", and make a conscious decision of using more balanced words like "sometimes" or "most of the time". When you have a negative way of thinking, it affects even the language you use. But you must make a conscious effort to alter this situation. By developing a language that promotes positivity, you will be sending a message to your brain to challenge its negative thinking patterns.

Explore the Connection between Your Emotions and Negative Thoughts

Whenever you experience a negative emotion, start by questioning the thought behind it. For instance, if you get anxious or depressed, go back to the thought that you just had. You will find that the thought was depressive in nature. For instance, you might have wondered why you have taken so long to achieve success or why you haven't settled, or you might have just thought that you're not good enough. Always monitor your thoughts and take notice of the negative thoughts. When you catch a negative thought early enough, it is easy to amend it. For example, instead of thinking, I'm not good enough by means of a mantra, you want to think, I'm a great person!

Choose Positive Explanations

No matter how your actions appear conventionally terrible, you can always rationalize them. For instance, if you had a child while you're still young, instead of looking at it as throwing your dreams away, look at it as bringing something new into the world. The same case applies to your thoughts. On the occasions that you experience negative thoughts, you want to find a positive or realistic explanation.

List down the Things That You're Grateful For

When you are battling negative thoughts, it is quite easy to overlook the many positive things about your life. To shift your mindset from negativity into positivity, you have to list down the things that you are grateful for. Some of the things that you ought to be grateful for include family, lovers, pets, and home. Whenever you fall short of your expectations, think about what you already have, and close the door to negative thinking patterns.

Practice Mindfulness

Instead of getting lost in the negative thoughts roaring in your mind, learn to shift your focus to the present. Pay direct attention to the things that you are doing at that moment, such as eating, drinking, and other daily activities.

Seek Guidance and Support

Don't bury yourself in negative thinking patterns. If you have tried in vain to get rid of your unhelpful thoughts, don't feel shy to reach out to an authority for help. They understand your problem probably more than you ever will. Get close to people too. You'd be amazed at the number of kind-hearted people out there ready to help you if you choose to want their help.

Chapter 28 Describe Automatic Thoughts and Intrusive Thoughts

What are Automatic and Intrusive Thoughts

CBT is based on the premise that it isn't the situation or circumstances that cause the condition, but the meaning assigned to these situations that lead us to experience depression or anxiety. The way we interpret a particular situation is what makes us slip into a negative state of mind. Often, the ideas that we hold about events or situations are impractical or blown out of proportion.

When these misleading notions are not challenged, they continue to grow stronger and lead to even more negativity. We assume it as our reality, which blocks us from perceiving things as they are and leading a fulfilling life. There is a tendency to overlook or ignore things that do not match our negative perception of events and situations. We continue to let these thoughts grow unhindered.

For instance, a person suffering from depression will think that he/she just can't go to the office today because nothing's going to be positive. Their thoughts operate from a sense of hopelessness. They end up believing what they think is true. So according to the person, nothing positive is bound to happen at work today, which means with their negative thought pattern there's absolutely no opportunity of knowing if this feeling is right or wrong. The person doesn't give himself/herself a chance to ascertain the veracity of their claims. Their thinking itself leads to the negative or unpleasant experience.

In the above example, the person stays at home and doesn't go to work. Thus he/she doesn't know whether their negative prediction had any clear basis. Such individuals sit at home thinking that they are an absolute failure and that they've let people down. They become angry with themselves and think about how incompetent and useless they are. This leads to the person feeling even worse than earlier, which results in more difficulty while attending office the following day. This causes a downward thinking, behavior and feeling spiral or a vicious circle that leads to several problems.

Where Do The Thoughts Originate?

According to the founder of CBT Aron Beck, the thoughts can be traced back to our childhood, when they become relatively rigid and involuntary. For instance, a child who may not have got enough attention and affection from the family but was encouraged to perform well academically may grow up with the notion that people have to be a success or do well every time. Such individuals will start believing that if they are not successful, people won't accept them. This may lead to the person putting excessive pressure on himself and slipping into depression if he fails to meet their own standards for success.

They may not experience the desired success due to something that's beyond their realm of control, which triggers the negative or dysfunctional thought. The person may believe that he/she isn't good enough or is a total failure. This will lead them to think they won't be accepted by others, and hence withdraw socially.

Cognitive behavioral therapy helps people to gain awareness of the fact that their mind is processing thoughts in a more skewed manner. It assists them in stepping out of their involuntary thought pattern and challenges these unfounded thoughts.

In the above instance, it challenges the person to assess her real-life instances for determining whether her thoughts are in congruence with reality. If something that has happened in their past or to someone else has indeed matched their perspective about the situation.

This helps them gain a greater realistic perspective, and they may end up gaining an opportunity to test the perspectives of other people by revealing their situation to close friends and family members.

There's no denying that negative things happen. However, when we are in a tough state of mind, our perspective and interpretations operate from a more biased plane. Thus we magnify the challenge we face. CBT assists people in modifying these skewed interpretations and helps them see things from a more balanced perspective.

CBT for Intrusive OCD Thoughts

Cognitive behavioral therapy points out that OCD or Obsessive Compulsive Disorder is when people misread intrusive thoughts or compelling urges as indications that harm will occur and they are directly responsible for their actions.

When it comes to treating OCD or intrusive thoughts through CBT, it helps individuals understand that their intrusive or disturbing obsessive thoughts are nothing but a result of anxiety than any real danger. OCD patients are gradually made to realize that they won't be affected or in danger if they don't give in to these thoughts.

People with OCD are desperately trying to avoid harm. Their solutions invariably end up becoming part of the issue. For instance, if you keep thinking about neutralizing your thoughts about stabbing someone, it only ends up increasing these intrusive thoughts.

The real issues, therefore, aren't these intrusive thoughts but the meaning assigned to them by an individual suffering from OCD. For example, you may experience a huge urge to act upon your intrusive thoughts or that you shouldn't have these thoughts in the first place. This places a huge level of threat, anxiety, and responsibility on you. In the above example, you'll stop meeting the person alone or stop stocking your kitchen with knives. You've succumbed to the fear. The fear is still alive, and further stops you from thinking that your fear is nothing but a skewed thought.

One of the most important aspects of using CBT to treat OCD or intrusive thoughts is that the therapist only functions as a facilitator and that it has to be practiced on your own.

Different therapists focus on different cognitive and behavioral attributes of OCD or intrusive thoughts. A cognitive focused approach will help you assess your thought patterns more keenly. For instance, you have thoughts about killing someone, which makes you feel that are a bad person for having these thoughts and you could act upon them. Your therapist will work with you to seek a different understanding of these distorted thoughts and give you an alternate technique for reacting to them.

If it's a more behavioral focused approach, it could be focused on educating yourself about how anxiety is felt by the body. It is about facing your fears and gradually taking on, and increasing the very activities you fear. For instance, if you suffer from social anxiety, your therapist will slowly get you to come out of your shell and participate in interactions on a smaller scale.

Where OCD or intrusive thoughts are concerned, the end goal of CBT is to change the brain's thought process or structure. Even if this sounds like a Herculean task, it isn't. Let's consider an example.

Let's assume you have lived in the United States of America all your life, and are used to a right-hand drive. There was no hassle of changing gears. Suddenly, you have to move to the United Kingdom, which is a left-hand drive. How will you manage?

To learn to drive left-handed, you have to unlearn right-handed driving. What makes the entire pursuit tough is that it has become a subconscious or almost involuntary process. If you've never driven left-handed, you'll initially have trouble getting used to sides, looking in the wrong direction and stepping out.

However, once you change or alter your actions and gradually get used to driving left-handed, you will learn to drive in the new direction. It comes with exposure, practice, and repetition. Repeated left handed driving experiences help you navigate corners, look in the right direction and step out with confidence. You practice this repeatedly until you've altered your brain structure.

Similarly, CBT seeks to question the veracity of your intrusive thoughts by consistent action, thus leading to a change in thought patterns. It transforms unrealistic and impractical intrusive thoughts into more real and evidence focused patterns. CBT will also help you restructure your behavior about avoiding certain things that lead to intrusive thoughts. For instance, if you experience repetitive thoughts about wanting to stab someone, you overcome avoiding holding knives or being alone with the person. Over a period of time, repeated new experiences help your brain learn to control anxiety experienced as a result of these irrational thoughts.

Setting Your Goal and Getting Started

Why Set Goals?

Goal setting is a fantastic form of self-motivation. When you set goals, you give yourself something to strive for. You have something you know you want and you are able to identify that in order to have a clear idea of what your actions are for. These goals can be anything, from getting a new job to learning a skill or meeting new people. Literally, anything you would like to achieve in life can be made into a goal. Just because anything can be made into a goal does not mean that there are no guidelines, however. By following some rules, and guidelines when setting your goals, you will learn to come up with goals that will be beneficial for you and help you change your behavior or life for the better. Ultimately, your goal should offer you some sort of benefit, whether

Bad Goals

Before getting into what rules there are to rule-setting, let's first analyze what makes a goal bad. There are three types of goals you should seek to avoid, as they are not conducive to a healthy mindset, nor are they effective for the right reasons. These goals are goals seeking to be in certain emotional states, goals that focus on the past, or goals that are rooted in negativity. Each of these types of goals is poorly formed or unproductive for various reasons.

Emotional States

Oftentimes, when people are setting goals for therapy, they think, "I want to feel happy in my own body and mind." At face value, this is a fine goal, but in reality, it is deeply rooted in feelings. However, feelings are constantly changing and fluctuating. This means that your goal may be achieved some of the time, but no one is every happy with themselves all of the time. You cannot help that sometimes; you will be disappointed or angry in yourself for something you did or a way you behaved. Because of the instability of emotions, they should be avoided as goals.

Focus on the past

People frequently also decide to set their goals as, "I want to get back to my old self," especially if their symptoms they are hoping to fix came up later in life. It is not unusual to miss the person you used to be but remember, that person is in the past. That person you used to do not go through the hard times you are hoping to get yourself out of, nor did that person have the knowledge you do now. CBT seeks to focus on the present and fix your mental health issues through actions, not by seeking out the past. The past can never be made present again, and you should never try to root your goals in returning to a past relationship, a past personality, or past feelings. You will always fail.

Negative or avoidant goals

Just as affirmations have to be kept positive in order to be effective, so too do goals. While the goal of, "I want to avoid feeling depressed," might sound like a reasonable goal, all this is doing is making you hyper-focused on avoiding the feelings of depression. By focusing on avoiding rather than on fixing the distressing symptoms, you are running from your problem. You also set yourself up for failure, because any time you fail and feel depressed, you will feel that depression compound onto itself as you collect another piece of evidence that you are as worthless and helpless as you thought you were. Ultimately, it is best to avoid setting goals with a focus on negativity or avoidance and instead focus on goals that are active instead.

SMART Goals

Now that you understand what not to do with your goals, it is time to learn what good goals consist of. It helps to remember that SMART goals are the most effective goals, with SMART being an acronym for specific, measurable, attainable, relevant, and timely. If you remember this acronym, you will be able to make your goals work for you.

Specific

When setting your goal, you want to be as specific with what you wish to attain as possible. The more specific you are, the clearer the picture you paint in your mind of what you want to achieve. There is a huge difference between saying you want to paint your room blue instead of specifying that you specifically want a light cerulean color, and likewise, there is a difference between saying you want to manage feelings of anger and angry outbursts, and stating that you want to reduce your outbursts over the course of the month. You went from a somewhat specific goal to one that gave an exact picture of what it will be.

Measurable

Just as more specific goals are desirable, having goals that are easily measurable is also crucial to set a good, productive goal. You need to be able to quantify what success looks like so you know exactly when you reach it, whether that is stating that you will write a certain amount of words a day, or save a certain amount of money. In the example of wanting to reduce anger outbursts, you could specify that you want to reduce the total number of times you react in anger by 40%. This goal now has a quantifiable definition of success.

Attainable

Your goal needs to be something you can actually reasonably complete. The easiest way to do this is to make sure your goal can easily be broken down into smaller goals to keep you motivated and moving forward. Every time you meet a goal, you feel encouraged, which keeps you moving forward, striving to complete more of your goals. This positive feedback loop reinforces the idea of meeting your goals, motivating you to start in the first place once your body and mind realize that doing so can be both beneficial and enjoyable. For example, if you set a goal of reducing angry outbursts, specifying smaller goals may make it more realistic for you to complete. You could say that you want to make it a point to have one less angry outburst than you did the day before every day. This gives you small milestone goals that will help keep you on track to attaining the whole goal.

Realistic

By making sure your goal is realistic, you avoid setting yourself up for failure. A realistic goal for one person is not going to be the same as a realistic goal for another; a fit, experienced mountain climber may be able to set and achieve a goal of climbing a huge mountain with a month to prepare, but the vast majority of people who do not mountain climb on a regular basis would likely find themselves falling out. Likewise, it can be realistic for one person to go running every day, but someone paralyzed from the neck down will never be able to attain it. Make sure your goal is reasonable and realistic to your specific situation. If you want to alleviate your anger issues and stop having angry outbursts, you have to set a realistic goal that recognizes that the process of changing your habits and mindsets.

Timed

Defining how long your goal will take gives you a clear goal with an end in sight. You give yourself a time to complete the goal by, and anything beyond that is deemed a failure. Keep in mind that you should give yourself a reasonable amount of time to complete your goal. Be realistic about your timeline and make sure it has at least some leeway for you to complete it while still giving yourself time as a motivator to work toward it. For example, if you want to reduce your angry outbursts, you decide on one month for the timeline to begin to see a reduction of 30%.

Examples of Goals

With an understanding of what a goal needs to be SMART, you will be ready to set goals that are beneficial to your mental wellbeing. Here are a few examples of goals.

Chapter 29 Understanding
Anxiety and Anxious Mind

If you picked up a copy of this book, it is most likely because you, or someone you love, is dealing with anxiety. You may know some of the symptoms, you may even have a diagnosis, but what you may not know is exactly what an anxious mind is and why it occurs.

Anxiety can strike anyone at any time, and while there are some risk factors involved, they don't always tell us who will be affected by this. Every year over 18% of the population will suffer from some form of an anxiety disorder, and yet only around 36% of those individuals will ever seek treatment or help. This leaves a large portion of the population suffering needlessly in silence, and feeling as if they are doomed by this disease.

Just like with most disorders, anxiety is highly treatable so long as the person who has it seeks out that help. But the problem with anxiety is that, oftentimes, it makes us too anxious to reach out to anyone, and so we end up in a cycle of fear.

One of the best ways to break this cycle is to start with baby steps, building ourselves up until we can overcome the anxiety long enough to ask for help. But how do we begin? And what do those baby steps look like?

Picking up this book was step one, and just by doing that, you are already in the process of overcoming your anxiety. It may not feel like anything has changed or that you have done anything dramatic, but you already have. So, let's dive straight in and look at what exactly anxiety is.

What is Anxiety?

Anxiety isn't necessarily a bad thing and is a very common and natural response to stressful situations. Maybe it's your first day of class, or you have an upcoming job interview or are going on the first day of work—all of these situations will make us feel anxious. This is our brain warning and preparing us for what is to come, and it typically benefits us by getting us ready to face a new situation, and it will subside as soon as the new experience is over.

But what happens when that anxiety prevents us from doing something new or it refuses to go away?

When we have a persistent feeling of being anxious, or when that anxiety interferes with our day to day life, then it goes beyond just a natural, normal occurrence. This is when someone will typically be diagnosed with having an anxiety disorder, and this is a common diagnosis that many people face.

You may hear people use the word "anxious" very frivolously, when in fact they mean to say that they are worried about something. "I'm so anxious about that upcoming test" would more appropriately be worded as "I'm so worried about that upcoming test." Making a distinction between worry and anxiety is extremely important, as one is normal, and one can be a serious problem.

The differences between worry and anxiety are very distinct and knowing which term to use in what situation can help you better identify if what you are feeling is normal or not. So, what should you look for to determine what exactly you are feeling?

- Being worried typically makes us feel mildly uncomfortable, whereas anxiety will make us extremely uncomfortable.

- Worry generally leads to mental problem solving, whereas anxiety causes a spiral with no solution.

- Worry is often based on realistic concerns, whereas anxiety is often based on nothing at all or mentally fabricated concerns.

- Worry can often be controlled and managed, but anxiety is harder to get rid of.

- Worry does not prevent us from living our life; anxiety will interfere personally and professionally.

- Worry is based on a very specific concern, whereas anxiety is more general.

- Worry is often something we think about mentally, whereas anxiety is felt mentally and physically.

Once you can identify if what you are feeling is worry or anxiety, you will be better equipped to handle it since each is treated differently. When you are worried about something, that is okay, and you will be able to handle it on your own and at the moment. Anxiety, on the other hand, is less easy to deal with and can oftentimes require professional help or even medication (which we will get into later on in this book).

What Does Anxiety Look Like?

Anxiety can be broken down into three main components: thoughts, sensations, and actions. These three components are experienced by those who are having healthy anxiety, but it is also experienced by those who are having unhealthy anxiety. The difference between the two comes down to this:

- Unhealthy anxiety happens and you do not know why.
- It is not a situation where most people would feel anxious.
- The anxiety lingers even after the situation has passed.
- You change the way you behave because of the anxiety.

If you can identify one or more of these during an anxiety attack, then you can know that you are experiencing unhealthy anxiety. So, what will that feel like to you?

Unhealthy Anxious Thoughts

The first component you will experience is the thoughts that plague your mind. These are thoughts that are unwanted and yet refuse to go away. You may be anxious that:

- Something you said or could say has upset someone.
- You do not have control over your environment or surroundings.
- That you are going to be late, or early, to a meeting.
- That something is about to go wrong.
- You have forgotten something important.
- The future may always be on your mind.
- You may feel like everyone is mad at you.
- Fear of embarrassment in public.
- Anxiety about making a mistake and being judged.
- You may feel anxious about feeling anxious.

These are all thoughts that something bad is going to happen, is happening, or has happened, and you cannot stop thinking about it. Whether or not there is any truth to the situation is irrelevant because, in your mind, it is very much real.

Unhealthy Anxiety Sensations

Anxiety has a physical component to it, as it is not just mental but can also create various physical sensations that are unpleasant and overwhelming. Some of the sensations that are associated with unhealthy anxiety include:

- Feeling like your heart is racing
- Heavy and quick breathing
- Sweaty palms
- Dizziness or lightheadedness
- Nausea or stomach pain
- Headaches and neck tension
- Shaking and shivering
- Difficulty falling asleep or staying asleep

The physical sensations are a big component because it makes it feel that much more real. When our bodies react in such a way, it tells us that what we are thinking is justified and it reaffirms that we need to be on alert and ready. These symptoms can also make us significantly more anxious because they are a signal to others that something is wrong with us. When it is just mental symptoms, we can hide those more easily, but if we are shaking and sweating, then someone may ask us what is wrong. This is why people with anxiety avoid being around others as it can make the cycle worse.

Unhealthy Anxiety Actions

When our mind and body tell us something is very wrong or something bad is about to happen, we will then respond by taking action to protect ourselves. Many of us have heard the term "fight-or-flight" before, and that is typically what occurs during an anxiety attack. Even if it isn't real, we now perceive a situation as being an attack on us, so we respond accordingly to escape danger. Some common unhealthy anxiety actions include:

- We may act out and snap at those around us.
- We may avoid certain situations.
- We may freeze up and be unable to function.
- We may hideaway in our homes and not go outside.
- We may cut off contact with loved ones.
- We may engage in unhealthy self-medicating behaviors such as consuming alcohol or drugs.
- We may become overly dependent on a spouse or loved one.

- We may avoid places that we think will trigger us such as public transportation, school, or even work.

This is the aspect of anxiety that interferes with our day-to-day life because we can no longer function normally. Instead of getting up each day and going to work, we become anxious to the point where basic tasks suddenly seem overwhelming. When anxiety gets to this point, that is when most of us start to realize that it is a serious problem that requires help.

Chapter 30 Causes of Fears, Anxiety and Panic Attacks

Anxiety

The time and how intense the feeling of anxiety is can sometimes be extensive as compared to the trigger. When the anxiety feeling exceeds, a person may experience increased blood pressure, and feelings of nausea may develop. When the feelings are this intense, they move from being normal anxiety to being an anxiety disorder.

A person that has an anxiety disorder is described as one with persistent concerns or thoughts that are intrusive. When a person cannot function normally due to anxious feelings, the person is considered to be suffering from an anxiety disorder.

Symptoms that an individual is suffering from an anxiety disorder

Various symptoms constitute to a person having an anxiety disorder. Some of these symptoms of the generalized disorder will include:

- An individual feeling restless and on edge
- When a person has feelings of worry that are uncontrollable
- When a person becomes increasingly irritable
- When a person experiences difficulties in concentration
- When a person starts experiencing difficulties falling asleep or sleeping in general

Although these may seem like normal symptoms that are common, individuals with a generalized anxiety disorder (GAD) experience them at extreme levels. With GAD, a person has vague, unsettling concerns and in some cases, severe anxiety that disrupts the daily functioning of the individual.

Common Causes of Anxiety Attacks

Causes of anxiety disorders are varied and complicated. Some causes may happen at the same time; others may lead to others, while others may not result in anxiety disorder unless another cause is present.

Some possible causes are:

- Environmental triggers such as challenges at work, family issues or relationship issues

- Genetics. Individuals that have family members that suffer from anxiety disorders could also experience them too.
- Medical triggers like symptoms of other diseases, the side effect of medication, the stress of an impending surgery, or recovery that has been prolonged.
- Brain chemistry meaning there is a misalignment of hormones and signals to the brain
- Withdrawing from taking an illicit substance may cause an intense impact on other triggers.

Physical and mental Clutter as a cause of Anxiety

Many people have accumulated many things in their lives that have caused clutter both in their physical environment and their minds. Clutter is a major cause of anxiety. A person bombards themselves with more material things than is necessary as well as having clutter in the mind. Living a simple life is a great way to avoid clutter, both mentally and physically, that would otherwise overwhelm you and cause you anxiety.

Many people want to please others, and they end up promising more than they can deliver. This will definitely cause you mental stress that makes you have anxious feelings. To prevent or avoid and even treat anxiety symptoms, people need to evaluate themselves and understand the clutter they are carrying and how to avoid it.

Fear

At the root of all mental disorders is one critical element known as fear. When it seizes your mind and body, you can only take one direction: down.

Fear is what will cause you to be scared of talking in front of an audience, what will hold you back from asking a member of the opposite sex out on a date, and what will make you shocked when you take an exam. But let's be clear. Fear is not wholly bad. Actually, it's a survival weapon that conditions us to perceive threats within our vicinity and react by either fighting back or escaping.

Anxiety is a type of fear that is tied to the thought of a threat or something terrible happening in the future as opposed to now. A person with an anxiety disorder battles intrusive and obsessive thoughts, as they try to make sense of both their emotions and thoughts.

What Makes You Afraid?

There are very many things that drive us into fear. The origins of our fear are, for the most part, rooted in our childhood experiences. If our guardians instill a fear of darkness in our childhood, we will grow into adults who still fear darkness until the moment we challenge that irrational fear. The first step toward overcoming fear is becoming aware of what you're afraid of and why.

What Makes You Anxious?

Anxiety is merely persistent fear, and it extends to your future. Having an anxiety disorder will surely harm your quality of life. You get into the mindset of seeing problems where there are none. Anxiety puts a quality of extremity to your life so that you're either withdrawn and isolated, or aggressive. Both extremes tend to stifle social cohesion.

How Does Fear Manifest?

When you are frightened or anxious, both your body and mind operate too quick. The following are some of the things that may happen thanks to fear and anxiety:

- Increased heartbeat

- Increased rate of breathing

- Weak muscles

- Profuse sweating

- Stomach pains

- Lack of concentration

- Lightheadedness

- A feeling of getting frozen

- Loss of appetite

- Hot and cold sweats

- Tense muscles

- Dry mouth

The physical symptoms of fear can be very frustrating, especially if you have no idea about the cause of your fear or anxiety. There are various triggers for fear and, sometimes, the brain keeps sending these messages even unnecessarily. You can only improve your capacity to understand your relationship with fear by raising your self-awareness.

Panic Attacks

Panic attack can be described as a sudden onset of extreme fear that continually increases for a couple of minutes. When you have a panic attack, you just experience overwhelming fear and anxiety coming over you, but you may not really understand what is happening.

You feel as if you are about to die from a heart attack due to the accelerated heart rate and other intense symptoms. However, you are experiencing the attack because of some psychological factors. A panic attack usually lasts for about 15 to 20 minutes, so the most important thing to do is to ride it out and wait for your body to go back to normal.

You may think that panic attacks are rare, but the truth is that they are quite common, with women being more susceptible than men. Though it is possible to experience a panic attack at any age, the majority of people tend to start feeling the effects between the ages of 25 and 30.

Symptoms

For you to be considered to be suffering from a panic attack, you must experience four or more of the following symptoms:

- Sweating

- Heart palpitations (increased heart rate)

- Trembling

- Shortness of breath

- Choking sensations

- Chest pain

- Feeling chilly or hot

- Light-headedness

- Abdominal discomfort

- Feeling like you are losing control

- Fear of dying

- Tingling or numb sensations

Causes

A panic attack is primarily the result of the adrenaline hormone flooding the body due to perceived danger. Notice that the key word here is perceived, which means that the problem is psychological in nature. As your adrenaline levels increase, you experience the above symptoms, but the hormone cannot stay at that high level for long, and soon drops down to normal.

Other factors that may contribute to your panic attacks include drinking too much coffee, stress, or failure to get adequate sleep. Maybe it was an impending exam or bad news about a loved one's health. Knowledge the cause will help you know what factors to avoid and reduce your anxiety about experiencing an attack when you least expect it.

Chapter 31 Identifying Obstacles Works with Thoughts, Worry, Fears and Anxiety

One of the greatest joys of my life is being able to help people overcome their anxiety and depression naturally. I'm sharing this knowledge with you today because I'd love to see you transform your life more easily than I did. I know you're going to love experiencing emotional health and happiness!

Yet, with anything that is precious and valuable in life, there are challenges and roadblocks to overcome along the way. So, of course there are also some problems and challenges with overcoming anxiety and depression naturally.

Let's discuss some of these challenges and roadblocks, so that you have a better understanding of the healing process.

Roadblock #1: Giving in to the conventional belief system

When we are feeling lost, scared and alone, it's very easy for us to believe the current conventional beliefs that say we are permanently damaged and we need medication to function normally.

Remember that we are programmed to believe those things by the multi-billion dollar corporations who are primarily concerned with marketing their medications. The well-being of consumers appears to be secondary to them.

Roadblock #2: Not having a mentor or guide

Since most of us were not taught how to resolve our feelings, it can often be a challenge to find our way through the muddle of our unresolved emotional issues on our own. Even if our intentions are good, we may feel lost and confused while trying to sort out complex issues by ourselves.

Fortunately, the truth about our life is actually simple. When we are guided appropriately, we can learn simple methods to find our way through the quagmire of unresolved issues and into the light of inner peace and happiness!

Roadblock #3: No support system for emotional health

Most of us didn't have healthy role models for emotional health as children. As a result, we generally copied the unhealthy family patterns we grew up with. When we don't have adequate support for getting out of our unhealthy family system, we can easily get distracted and lose track of our goals.

Learning how to find support for our personal growth can make all the difference in achieving health and happiness. By developing a healthy support system, we can always have someone to talk to on the days that we really need support for our healing journey.

Roadblock #4: Having a lack of patience, commitment and persistence

Facing the truth about your life does have its challenges. Without these important qualities, it's easy to get derailed by the twists and turns that come on our journey to emotional health.

When we are working through difficult life issues, we'll probably have days where our emotions feel overwhelming. But when we practice our patience, commitment and persistence, often those challenging days mark the beginning of an amazing breakthrough in our lives.

Roadblock #5: Giving up before you complete the journey

Some people start the process and then decide it's too hard or it takes too long, so they go back to their old behaviors and wonder why their life isn't working.

If we give up before we get to emotional health and happiness, we miss out on experiencing the amazing happiness and inner peace that are possible.

Chapter 32 Triumph Over Anger and Depression

Anger usually occurs as a natural response to feeling attacked, frustrated, or even being humiliated. It is human nature to get angry. The fury, therefore, is not a bad feeling per se, because, at times, it can prove to be very useful. How is this even possible? Anger can open one's mind and help them identify their problems, which could drive one to get motivated to make a change, which could help in molding their lives.

When is Anger a Problem?

Anger, as we have just seen, is normal in life. The problem only comes in when one cannot manage their anger, and it causes harm to people around them or even themselves.

How does one notice when their anger is becoming harmful? When one starts expressing anger through unhelpful or destructive behavior, or even when one's mental and physical health starts deteriorating. That's when one knows that the situation is getting out of hand.

It is the way a person behaves that determines whether or not they have problems with their anger. If the way they act affects their life or relationships, then there is a problem, and they should think about getting some support or treatment.

What is Unhelpful Angry Behavior?

Anger may be familiar to everyone, but people usually express their rage in entirely different ways. How one behaves when they are angry depends on how much control they have over their feelings. People who have less control over their emotions tend to have some unhelpful angry behaviors. These are behaviors that cause damage to themselves or even damage to people or things around them. They include:

Inward Aggression

This is where one directs their anger towards themselves. Some of the behaviors here may include telling oneself that they hate themselves, denying themselves, or even cutting themselves off the world.

Non-Violent or Passive Aggression

In this case, one does not direct their anger anywhere; rather, they stick with the feeling in them. Some of the behaviors here may include ignoring people, refusing to speak to people, refusing to do tasks, or even deliberately doing chores poorly or late. These types of behaviors are usually the worst ways to approach such situations. They may seem less destructive and harmful, but they do not relieve one of the heavy burdens that are causing them to be angry.

Preparation

Weigh Your Options

In life, many things may be out of one's control. These things vary from the weather, the past, other people, intrusive thoughts, physical sensations, and one's own emotions. Despite all these, the power to choose is always disposable to any human. Even though one might not be able to control the weather, one can decide whether or not to wear heavy clothing. One can also choose how to respond to other people.

The first step, therefore, in dealing with anger is to recognize a choice.

1. A "Should" Rule is Broken

Everybody has some rules and expectations for one's behavior, and also for other people's behavior. Some of these rules include, "I should be able to do this," "She should not treat me like this," and, "They should stay out of my way." Unfortunately, no one has control over someone else's actions. Therefore, these rules are always bound to be broken, and people may get in one's way. This can result in anger, guilt, and pressure.

It is, therefore, essential to the first break these "should" rules to fight this anger. The first step to make in breaking these rules is to accept the reality of life that someone usually has very little control over other people's lives. The next step is for one to choose a direction based on one's values. How does one know their values? One can identify their values by what angers them, frustrates them, or even enrages them. For example, let's take the rule of "They should stay out of my way." This rule may mean the values of communication, progress, or even cooperation. What do these values mean to someone? Does one have control over them?

Finally, one can act by their values. To help with this, here are two questions one should ask themselves:

- What does one want in the long run?
- What constructive steps can one take in that direction?

2. What Hurts?

The second step is to find the real cause of pain or fear after breaking the rules. These rules usually do not mean the same as one's body. This is because some states of being can hurt one's self-esteem more than others.

To understand this better, let's take the example of Susan, who expects that no one should talk ill of her. Then suddenly John comes up to her and says all manner of things to her. This, therefore, makes Susan enraged. In such a scenario, Susan should ask herself what hurts her. The answer to this question will bring out a general belief about John and herself. She will think that "John is rude," "She is powerless," or even that "She is being made the victim." All these thoughts may hurt her. What may even hurt her most is that she has no control over John's behavior.

Once she has noted that she has no control, she may now consider seeing John's words as a mere opinion rather than an insult. This will make her not see herself as a victim, but as a person just receiving a piece of someone else's mind about herself.

3. Hot Thoughts.

After one has identified what really hurts them, it is now time to identify and, most importantly, replace the hot, anger-driven, and reactive thoughts with more level-headed, more relaxed, and reflective thoughts. Here are some fresh ideas that may be of importance to someone:

Hot thought: "How mean can he be!"

A cool thought: "He thinks he is so caring."

Hot thought: "They are stupid!"

A cool thought: "They are just human."

4. Anger

All the above steps, as one may have noticed, relate to the thoughts. This is because one has first to tackle the ideas before now getting to the emotion. In this step, therefore, one is going to respond to the anger arousal itself. There are three ways that one can follow to respond to this emotion:

- One may indulge in relaxation. This relaxation can come in many forms, like enjoying some music, practicing some progressive muscle relaxation like yoga, and also visualization.

- One may also use that feeling to do some constructive work. When one is angry, there is usually a large amount of energy that one uses at that time. This is the reason that when angry, one can break down things that they would never break when calm. Imagine, therefore, how much that energy would do for someone if just directed to some constructive work.

- One may also try to redefine anger when one gets angry. What does this mean? Once a person is angry, one can try to remind themselves of how anger is a problem that fuels aggression and can cause harm to loved ones and even oneself.

5. Moral Disengagement

In simple words, this step will help one examine the beliefs that turn anger into aggression. These beliefs usually act as mere excuses or justification for destructive acts. Some of these beliefs include "I don't care," "This is the only way I can get my point across," or even "It is high time they recognize me." These beliefs need to be identified early enough and gotten rid of before they can con one into throwing one's morals aside. One sure way of getting rid of them is by reminding oneself of the cost of such beliefs and the advantages of striving for understanding.

6. Aggression

In this step, one now needs to examine the behaviors that arise from aggression and try to fight them. Fighting these behaviors can be achieved if one calms down and puts themselves in the other person's shoes. This will help one understand why the other person is acting in such a manner, what they may be feeling, or even what they may be thinking. This approach will help to:

- Decrease the anger for all parties involved.

- Increase the chance of having a reasonable conversation with the parties involved, and thus everybody is heard.

7. Outcome

The final step of this procedure is to reduce resentment towards others, and also guilt towards oneself.

Treating depression with cognitive behavioral therapy.

What is depression?

Depression is a feeling of severe despondency and dejection. In life, it is only natural for one to feel less than a hundred percent at times. This is like when one is battling with drug addiction or has relationship problems. However, this low feeling sometimes gets a hold of one's life and won't go. This is what we call depression. Depression can make one feel lonely and hopeless.

If one has such feelings, there is light at the end of the tunnel. Cognitive Behavioral Therapy is here to restore one's hope in life. This is because it can help one think more healthily, and also help in overcoming a particular addiction.

Before getting more in-depth with the advantages of CBT on a depressed person, let's first look at the different types of depression.

Types of Depression

Depressions are of various kinds. They can either occur alone or concurrently with an addiction. The best thing, however, is that the following categories are treatable through using CBT.

Major Depression

This disorder occurs when one feels depressed most of the time for most days of the week. Some of the symptoms associated with this disorder are:

- Weight loss or weight gain

- Being tired often

- Trouble getting sleep

- Thoughts of suicide

- Concentration problems

- Feeling restless or agitated

If you experience five or more of the above signs on most days for two weeks or longer, then they have this disorder.

Persistent Depressive Disorder (PDD)

This type of depression usually lasts for two years or even longer. The symptoms associated with the disorder include:

- Sleeping too much or too little

- Fatigue

- Low self-esteem

Bipolar Disorder

A person with such a disorder usually experiences mood episodes that range from extremes of high energy with an "up" mood to low periods.

How CBT Helps with Negative Thoughts of Depression

The cognitive-behavioral therapy understands that when one has low moods, they tend to have negative thinking. This negative thinking usually brings cases of hopelessness, depression, and can also lead to a change in behavior.

CBT, therefore, works to help with the patterns of behavior that need to be changed. In short, it works to recalibrate the part of the brain that keeps a tight hold on happy thoughts.

Five CBT Techniques to Counteract the Negative Thinking of Depression

There are several techniques that one can follow to help with fighting off negative thoughts. Before starting these steps, one should make sure that they are ready to undertake them and should keep track of themselves. Here are some of the steps:

Locate the Problem and Brainstorm for Solutions

The first step is to discover the cause of the problem. This step requires one to talk with one's inner self. Once the idea of what the problem might be dawning on you, write it down in simple words. Then write down a list of things that one can do to improve the problem.

Write Self-Statements to Counteract Negative Thoughts

Once the cause of the problem has been discovered, it is now time to identify the negative thoughts that seem to pop up in one's brain every time. Write self-statements to counteract each foul view. These self-statements are statements that are going to stuff up the negative thoughts. One should always recall all their self-statements and repeat them back to themselves every time a negative thought pops up. However, these self-statements should continually be refreshed because they can, at times, be too routine.

Find New Opportunities to Think Positive Thoughts

Michael is a person who always sees the negative part of people before noticing their bright side. These people, more often than not, usually get depressed quickly. To remedy this, they should always change their thinking and think positively. This, for example, in the case of Michael, can be like first noticing and appreciating how neat people are. This type of thinking can be tough to change. Here are some of the recommended ways that one can adjust to such thinking;

- Set one's phone to remind them to reframe their minds to something positive.

- Pairing up with someone who is working on this same technique. This will make one have positive thoughts, and also get to enjoy them with someone else.

Finish Each Day by Visualizing Its Best Parts

After each day, one can write down the most exciting events of the day and try to remember them. Sharing such moments online can even help one form new associations, and also thinking ways that can prove to be very helpful.

Learn to Accept Disappointment as a Normal Part of Life

In life, disappointment is bound to come one's way. How one deals or behaves after a disappointing event determines how fast one is going to move forward. Take, for example, John, who just lost a job interview. This is a thing that can happen to anyone. The way he responds to this situation will determine how fast he is going to move forward. If he starts getting the thoughts of "I am a failure," "The world is so unfair to me," or even "I will never succeed in life," then he is moving in the wrong direction. Later, he can write some things he has learned from the experience and things he can do to remedy it next time.

Chapter 33 Challenging Automatic and Intrusive Thoughts

Cognitive reconstruction in CBT for anxiety

Cognitive reconstruction also referred to as thought challenging involves a process whereby we simply challenge the patterns yielding to negative thoughts. The goal of doing this is to make you anxious and then replacing these patterns with realistic and positive thinking. Here are the steps involved in doing this are;

Identification of the negative thoughts

People suffering from anxiety disorders perceive situations that we see to be normal as very dangerous. For example, germ phobia can make someone to really find it life-threatening when shaking another person's hands. In as much as it may appear easy to see the irrational fears, it can, however, be difficult to identify your own irrational and scary thoughts. Therefore, the most preferred strategy is by asking yourself to roll back to determine your thoughts at the moment the anxiety feeling started. You should be guided on how to do this step by step by your therapist.

Challenging the negative thoughts in you

You have already identified the thoughts that make you anxious. Therefore, your therapist will provide you with a guide on how you can evaluate the thoughts that provoke your anxiety. This will basically involve trying to question the evidence of thoughts that frighten you, analyzing of beliefs you feel are unhelpful and then trying to test the reality of negative predictions. In order to effectively challenge your negative thoughts, you can conduct experiments, weigh the advantages and disadvantages of worrying and then try to determine the realistic chances of the possibilities of what you are worrying or anxious about.

Negative thinking is something that everyone does from time to time, however, those suffering from depression are at risk for being controlled by it. It influences your decisions and has a major impact on your mood. When you fall into negative thinking, it also makes it a lot harder to fight your depression, so it is important to get this type of thinking under control.

The first step is identifying your negative thoughts so that you can work to counter them and turn them into something positive. When you start to feel emotions like anger, frustration, irritability, depressed mood or anxiousness, take a minute to think about why you feel this way. This gives you a minute to reflect on what is happening and what is causing these emotions. You want to do four things what you are experiencing negative emotions to identify your negative thoughts and overcome them:

Test Reality

Test the reality of your negative thoughts by asking yourself the following:

• What evidence supports my current thinking?

• Am I jumping to a negative conclusion?

• Are my thoughts interpretations or are they factual?

• How can I determine if these thoughts are true?

Seek Alternative Explanations

Ask yourself these questions to see if there are alternative explanations:

• What could this mean?

- What other ways can I explore this situation?

- How would I see this situation if I were being positive?

Put it in Perspective

Put your thinking and feelings in perspective by asking yourself these questions:

- Is this situation really as bad as I see it?

- What great things can happen in this situation?

- What is good about this situation?

- Will this situation even matter in five years?

- How likely is something bad to happen and what is the worst that can happen?

- What is likely to happen?

Utilize Goal-Directed Thinking

Ask yourself the following questions to take advantage of goal-directed thinking:

- Are my thoughts helping me to reach my goals?

- Can I learn something from this situation?

- What can I do to solve the problem?

These four steps allow you to work through your negative thoughts so that you can explore their origin so that you can prevent them in the future. When you recognize negative thoughts and take the time to address them, you are working toward thinking more positively naturally. This means that you will be less likely to experience negative thoughts in the future. You will gain a new perspective and be able to use it effectively to transform your thoughts into something that helps you to move forward.

There are four other things that you can do to work toward challenging your negative thoughts and feelings. Consider the following methods for helping you to think more positively:

• Talk it out: Find someone who you trust who knows you well and talk about your negative thoughts and feelings. The key to talking about it with someone else is to get a fresh perspective to help you understand, recognize and undo your negative thinking.

• Get relaxed: Take a few minutes each day and do something relaxing that allows you to get inside your own head and consider your thoughts. Things like meditation and yoga are popular options because they help you to open your mind so that you can focus on the thoughts that you are having.

• Improve your physical health: When you are working on your physical health, this often boosts your confidence. Those with more confidence tend to naturally think more positively. This also gives you positive things in your life to focus on.

• Write it down: When you are having negative thoughts, take a minute to write them down. You can look at them later in the day to determine where your negative thoughts were coming from. This will allow you to make the changes necessary to become a more positive person. It also helps you to identify that factors that cause you to have negative thoughts.

Replacing the negative thoughts

Now that the negative distortions and irrational predictions have been identified, it is time now you replace such thoughts with more positive and accurate thoughts. In such situations, you can let your therapist assist you in developing for you new realistic thoughts or motivating statements that you can always refer to when faced with a tough situation that normally makes you anxious.

Let's consider the following examples: Bill is afraid of taking a subway because he feels that he will pass out, and everybody in the sub will think that he is crazy. He decides to go for therapy. The therapist, in turn, asked him to think and write down his negative thoughts and then try to identify the cognitive distortions or the errors that he feels are in his thinking. After doing this, the therapist told him to develop a rational interpretation of his thoughts.

Challenging the Negative Thoughts in You

The first thought (negative): I will faint while on the subway. What will happen if that happens?

Cognitive distortion: Prediction of the worst

Realistic thinking: This has never happened to me. This will not happen.

ii. The second negative thought: It will really be terrible if I pass out

Cognitive distortion: Things are already blowing out of control

Realistic thinking: The subway has its own medics and therefore if I faint, that will not be terrible. The third negative thought: Other people will definitely think of me as crazy

Cognitive distortion: You are already jumping into conclusions

Realistic thinking: People will be concerned to see that I get okay

Replacing the negative thoughts, however, is not easy. This is because negative thinking forms part and parcel of a prolonged thinking pattern and will require time and practice to break this bad habit. For this reason, cognitive behavioral therapy also includes practicing where you are required to as well as practice while at home.

Chapter 34 Taking Action Against Anxiety

When you are stuck in depression, you may feel like you cannot progress.

What are Action Plans?

Action plans are another way to engage in problem-solving. These involve six specific questions that you must consider in regards to whatever it is that you are trying to get, and if you can answer them, you have a pretty good plan to get what you need.

These action plans can help you understand what comes next when you are trying to get what you want. By breaking down your goal into manageable steps, you will understand how to get there without getting overwhelmed.

The whole purpose of action plans, beyond just creating steps, is to push you from someone who has things that happen to you into a doer. You are no longer going to be a passive part of your life—instead, you are learning how to take action and do something.

How do Action Plans Help Depression?

When you suffer from depression, you likely feel like you are all caught up in the world around you, feeling like there is little to no point in moving on. You do not see the point in changing your own behaviors because you feel like it will not matter anyway.

You may even be too overwhelmed to actually tackle your problem in the first place. This can be problematic for you if stress is one of your biggest depression triggers. However, you do not have to be overwhelmed any longer. As you come up with an action plan, you create manageable steps to achieving what you want. Because the steps will be smaller and more manageable than the entire goal as a whole, you will not feel nearly as intimidated by it. This means that you will have more luck actually engaging with your action plan and getting what you want.

Steps to Creating Action Plans

When it comes time to create an action plan, you must first start off with a problem. After all, your action plan would not be complete without a problem that it seeks to solve, or a goal that you wish to achieve. Perhaps you are stressed about school and wish to alleviate that stress. Maybe you stress because you have a tendency to snap at your children, and the fact that you do snap at them just makes your stress level worsen. Those are both emotional issues, which action plans can help you with. You can develop strategies to lessen the stress. However, you can also create action plans in other contexts as well.

Perhaps you want to lose some weight or develop a new skill. Your action plan can help you with that. You might want to learn how to be more social, which can also be done through action planning. You may even need to find a new job or wish to get into a relationship with someone else. That is also entirely possible for you to achieve with action plans.

Ultimately, your action plan is going to help you achieve whatever it is you desire. Your action plan is going to ask you six specific questions that can help you really flesh out what it is you want. As you go through these six questions, you will get a better understanding of everything that your action goal entails.

First, identify what you want and write it down. This is anything you want. In this case, let's use the example of wanting to get a new job. That is something that is nice and concrete, making it easy to understand.

Next, you are going to ask yourself why it is important. In this case, you need a new job. This is relatively simple to understand why you would need one— everyone needs money. You may need the pay raise that would come with a new job, or perhaps you are miserable at your current job and need out for your own sanity. Maybe your job is something boring to you, and you want to pursue a field that will make you happier. You may even want to relocate, but relocating requires you to first land a job wherever you would like to move.

Now, ask yourself when you want this to happen. This is creating a timeline for your action. This is important because if you never have a timeline for it, you are not going to feel particularly pressured to attempt to get your desired result. When you do have a timeline, however, you are able to keep yourself accountable. This accountability can be the difference between failing or succeeding.

Third, ask what you need in order to achieve your goal. Do you need any new skills to get that new job you want? Is going back to college or getting a new certification necessary? Do you need a car that will enable you to get to and from your dream job? Do you need to relocate? Will you need a change in the wardrobe to match the new job's company culture?

Fourth, identify if you need any intervention from other people, or if you could benefit from asking someone else to help. Do you have any references for that job you want? Is there anyone you can talk to that already works for the company that you want to work for that can give you an idea of what to expect? Do you need a babysitter for kids while you interview or start at your new job?

Fifth, you need to ask yourself how you will know that you have actually achieved the goal. In this case, that is quite simple: You will have a new job. Sometimes, however, things are not as clear. You may want to reduce your depression's effect on you, and that is something that can be difficult to really measure. However, you can say that you know you have achieved that goal when you are able to face your daily responsibilities most of the time.

Lastly, you now start planning out the steps. What are the steps you will need to reach your goal? With applying for a job, it is relatively simple; once more— you will need to locate jobs that are hiring at that moment, create a resume and cover letter, ensure you have references, apply, interview, and accept a job offer. When you want to alleviate some of your depressive symptoms, you may say that you will engage in therapy, increase your healthy behaviors, take antidepressants, and find any other ways that you could help alleviate those depressive symptoms.

With all of your actions lined up for you to consider, you are able to see exactly what your goal is going to require. When you are suffering from depression, you want your goals to be as clear-cut as possible, allowing you to take action in a way that does not seem intimidating to you. After all, if you feel like the process is insurmountable or like you cannot succeed because you do not know where to start, you are not likely to get very far.

To help you with your action planning, it can help to create a list or a graphic that makes everything visible for you as you go through the planning period. As you finish the action plan graphic, you will be able to see everything in front of you as you organize it, which ensures that you do not forget parts along the way. You will have all of your brainstorming right in front of you so you can get it right the first time.

When you create a web-like the above one, you are actively putting in the effort necessary to plan. Sometimes, that planning can be enough to spur you into action, as you feel like going through the effort and writing it down commits you to finish. After all, why would you have gone through that effort if you were not going to use it? If you do not want to waste time, you will be committed to acting. This is frequently known as the sunk-cost fallacy, where you feel like the resources you have invested justify following the process through to the end. Usually, this is something that can be detrimental to you, particularly if you have put in money to a business and are now at risk of losing it if you continue to invest and having your credit ruined, or if you stick out a relationship in which you are miserable because you have been together for too long to not try. However, when you use an action plan to trigger that, you can use what is usually a negative as a positive instead, taking advantage of the way that minds tend to function and using it to your benefit.

Chapter 35 Releasing Control

One of the biggest benefits behind managing anxiety with CBT is that you are managing your anxiety in a natural way. While some forms of anxiety will require medication, some people find that creating a natural management plan is much easier and feels more aligned with them and their needs. With that being said, CBT is not the only way that you can manage your anxiety in a natural manner that will help improve your symptoms and support you with feeling your best. If you want to really approach your anxiety with a full system for helping you not only manage but also heal and cure your anxiety, incorporating some alternative natural approaches can be helpful, too.

When it comes to anxiety, specifically, there are several things you can do to help you begin to manage your anxiety more effectively. Most of these methods are lifestyle methods, although some of them can be targeted toward anxiety itself, too. The eight things that you can do that will really help you navigate your anxiety more effectively and naturally heal yourself include: exercise, avoiding anxiety-inducing substances, resting, meditating, improving your diet, teas, and herbs, aromatherapy, and taking the pressure off of yourself.

Maintain Regular Exercise

Exercise is necessary for your general wellbeing, yet many people fail to incorporate enough exercise into their everyday routine. Ideally, you should be engaging in at least 30 minutes of moderate exercise every single day, as well as moving your body around at least once per hour. Ensuring that you engage in enough movement and exercise will help you use up any adrenaline and cortisol that your body may produce as a byproduct of your anxiety. As well, it will help naturally regulate your hormones and chemicals to ensure that your hormonal system is functioning more effectively. For some people, this can translate to experiencing less anxiety overall because their system functions more effectively as a result of their exercise.

In addition to helping you regulate your hormones and chemicals within your body, exercise can also release endorphins into your system that actually support you in staying more relaxed and navigating anxiety, as well as other emotions more effectively. These endorphins can be found in your body for up to several hours after working out, meaning that one single workout session can help regulate your hormones, chemicals, and emotions for several hours. If you continue working out on a consistent basis, this can translate to ongoing, long-term relief from your anxiety symptoms.

Avoid Alcohol, Cigarettes, and Caffeine

Alcohol is known for being a natural sedative, which means that it can support you with relaxing yourself from anxiety. One single glass of wine or a shot of whiskey can calm your nerves and support you with navigating your anxiety more effectively – at first. However, as soon as the buzz from that small portion of alcohol wears off, your anxiety can come back far stronger and more intense than ever. Attempting to treat your anxiety with alcohol can lead to alcoholism while also exacerbating the symptoms of your anxiety and making you feel even worse in the long run.

Cigarettes are also known for exacerbating your anxiety by worsening your risk of anxiety over time. Although smoking a cigarette when you are actively feeling stressed might seem to calm you down, the reality is that research has shown that long-term cigarette usage actually massively increases your risk for problematic anxiety symptoms. As well, nicotine itself is said to increase your anxiety symptoms, which means that you may actually find yourself feeling even worse after a cigarette.

Lastly, caffeine is known as a stimulant and can massively aggravate your anxiety. If you are drinking caffeine on a regular basis, and you find yourself dealing with problematic anxiety, you need to start cutting back on caffeine or eliminating it entirely. Releasing caffeine from your daily drinking ritual will massively support you with avoiding unwanted anxiety and allowing yourself to experience more calmness in your life.

Create A Stronger Rest Routine

People who experience chronic or problematic anxiety often report that they tend to experience a strange or inconsistent sleep schedule. For some people, the strange or inconsistent sleep schedule might be the result of their anxiety itself, whereas others might find that the schedule is more closely linked to their lifestyle and leads to the experience of anxiety. If you are trying to overcome anxiety in your life, learning how to navigate a healthier rest cycle will be important to your wellbeing. The more you can support yourself in navigating a healthier rest cycle, the more you will find yourself experiencing freedom from your anxiety.

Ideally, you should have a strong bedtime routine as well as plenty of sleep throughout each night to support you with experiencing healthier rest cycles and more support from your sleep. With both in place, you will likely find yourself experiencing significant relief from your anxiety.

For your bedtime routine, try avoiding using your phone, tablet, or any other device with a screen for at least 30-45 minutes before bed. As well, do not read or watch television in bed or otherwise engage in active activities in your bed as this can lead to you associating your bed with a space to be active and awake. You should also try incorporating some relaxing pre-bedtime routines, like drinking a relaxing tea, journaling, taking a warm bath, or doing a gentle yoga practice. These types of calming experiences will help you release your stress, calm your mind, and prepare yourself for a good night's sleep.

You should also make sure that you are going to bed at a reasonable hour and waking up 7-9 hours later, which is the recommended amount of sleep for the average adult. Getting a proper amount of sleep and waking up on time will ensure that you are well-rested when you wake up and that you have not overslept, too.

Practice Meditating

Meditation is one of the most powerful things you can do to help you naturally relieve anxiety, and it can also support you with active anxiety attacks or bouts of anxiety if you find yourself struggling. Having a regular meditation practice will support you with relaxing yourself in between anxiety, and with managing your anxiety more effectively and completely when it spikes. Your main goal with meditation is to relax your mind and let yourself experience peace, so naturally, this can have a positive and healthy impact on your mind, especially when you are navigating anxiety. In fact, some studies have shown that those who meditate on a consistent basis experience massive relief from things such as anxiety, stress, worry, and even depression and other emotional or mental disorders.

If you are new to meditation, getting into the practice of meditating for just 10-15 minutes per day can have a huge impact on helping you relieve yourself from anxiety. However, you should be focused on working your way up to meditating for about 30 minutes a day, as this is what John Hopkins medical research center recommends as being the best length of time for relief from anxiety, as well as depression. You should practice meditating whether you feel anxious or not, as keeping a healthy and ongoing meditation practice will support you in fully overcoming anxiety in the long run. Think of this as being similar to practicing CBT techniques outside of anxiety before bringing them into your anxiety cycle: the more you practice, the better you get, and the more effective it will be at helping you in your times of need.

If you struggle to meditate, following a guided meditation on YouTube can be helpful in allowing you to meditate more effectively. You may also want to turn meditation into more of a ritual where you involve gentle music, a comfortable pillow and blanket, and some soothing aromatherapy or candles to help set the tone. The more you can relax and let your mind experience relief, the more peace you will experience in your life.

Improve Your Diet

Much like alcohol, cigarettes, and caffeine can impact your anxiety, and your diet can actually impact your anxiety, too. Your diet can increase symptoms of anxiety in many ways. If you are not eating enough or you are not eating well enough, your body can become stressed from your unhealthy dietary styles and can actually increase your levels of cortisol in your body, which can lead to symptoms of anxiety. As well, some foods are naturally energizing and can lead to you having anxiety as a result of these boosted energies. Learning to avoid any form of natural stimulants can be helpful in supporting you with navigating your anxiety more effectively.

The foods you need to avoid include any that have been processed or that are laced in chemicals such as artificial flavors, colors, or preservatives. You also need to avoid letting your blood sugars drop too low or letting yourself get dehydrated, as these can both lead to the increase of anxiety within your body. In addition to that, avoid high sugar diets and stimulating foods and herbs like ginseng, chocolate (which can contain caffeine), and any other number of herbs or supplements that may be stimulating in nature.

Eating a diet that is healthy and rich in complex carbohydrates, vegetables, fruits, and lean proteins can help you support yourself with overcoming anxiety more effectively. You can also focus on eating foods that are known for supporting your brain health, such as those that are rich in fatty omega-3 acids, like fish, as these can support your brain is having an easier time creating new neural pathways. Some studies suggest that this may make it easier for you to be more resilient toward anxiety and more effective in implementing your new CBT practices.

Use Calming Teas and Herbs

Just like certain herbs can stimulate you, others can actually help you relax, too. Learning how to use tea and herbs to support you in relaxing yourself can be helpful in allowing you to bring down your energy levels and offset your anxiety naturally. Some people like to drink calming teas on a regular basis, whereas others might drink them exclusively around the time that they are feeling anxious so that they can experience relief. Ideally, you should drink calming teas on an ongoing basis. However, either method will support you in naturally bringing down your energy levels and calming yourself from anxiety.

There are seven incredible natural loose leaf teas you can use that will really help you when it comes to bringing down your anxiety levels. These seven include peppermint tea, chamomile tea, lemon balm tea, passionflower tea, green tea, rose tea, and lavender tea. Each of these is known for having various constituents in it that can help you naturally relieve yourself of anxiety, while often also supporting you in uplifting any depression that you may be experiencing.

When it comes to drinking teas or using herbs to support you in navigating anxiety, it is important that you are aware of which ones might worsen your symptoms. Many teas contain higher levels of caffeine, which may or may not offset your anxiety. Some people can handle lightly caffeinated teas, whereas other people might find themselves feeling far too sensitive to even small amounts of caffeine. You can test to see where you fall on this scale. With that being said, avoid black teas and Pu-erh teas as they are known for having more caffeine than coffee, which can make them terrible for managing anxiety. White tea, mate, green tea, and oolong tea can all be used instead of caffeinated beverages and may be gentle enough that they do not stimulate your anxiety, but they do give you a slight boost in energy.

Try Aromatherapy

Aromatherapy has been said to be a powerful tool for helping navigate many different ailments, including anxiety. If you are experiencing troubling anxiety, using aromatherapy may help you support yourself in lowering your anxiety levels and supporting yourself with feeling more at peace in your life. When using aromatherapy, there are a few things that you should know to make sure that you get the most out of your experience while also staying safe.

The first thing you need to know is that aromatherapy works on two levels. The first level is by infusing the constituents of the oil with your body, meaning that it works similarly to tea. The same way that certain elements of tea encourage you to relax in the way that certain elements of aromatherapy blends will encourage you to relax, too. The other way that aromatherapy can help you is through olfaction. Olfaction is a process whereby you smell something, and it activates a part of your limbic system, which essentially means that it triggers certain memories. When certain aromatherapy blends have the capacity to activate your more peaceful memories, it can support you with navigating anxiety more effectively.

Before you begin using aromatherapy, make sure that you purchase your oils from a high-quality source that you trust completely. As well, make sure that you are aware of what oils are safe and are not safe for you to use. Sometimes, essential oils can be dangerous for certain people with certain conditions or for pets, so you need to make sure that the oils you use are safe for yourself and everyone in your home. If you find that the oil you want to use is not safe, do not use it at all as it can cause problems for you or the members of your family rather quickly.

The oils that you can consider using to support you with navigating anxiety include lavender oil, rose oil, vetiver oil, ylang-ylang oil, frankincense oil, geranium oil, jasmine oil, and chamomile oil. All eight of these are known for supporting people with reducing their symptoms of anxiety and experiencing greater calm and peace in their lives.

Release the Pressure From Yourself

The last and sometimes most powerful thing you can do for yourself when you are dealing with anxiety and trying to overcome it naturally releases the pressure for yourself. As a species, we have a tendency to put a massive amount of pressure on ourselves through the expectations that we tend to have on ourselves in life. You may be combining your own high expectations with the expectations that other people have of you, leading to you overwhelming yourself with expectations that you cannot meet. If you are overwhelmed by the expectations that you have placed on yourself, or that you feel others have placed on you, you need to practice taking the pressure off and giving yourself space for a while.

Releasing the pressure from yourself can be difficult, especially if you have had high expectations of yourself for quite some time. You might find yourself struggling to fully release the pressure and let yourself be patient and gentle with yourself, even if you have set the intention to do so. In this case, exercising the practice of CBT on your tendency to put pressure on yourself may be ideal as you learn to change your perspective and give yourself permission to slow down in life and take some of the stuff off of your plate.

The more you can be gentle and patient with yourself, the more you are going to find yourself experiencing peace from your anxiety. Many people are surprised to learn that when they stop expecting so much of themselves, suddenly they have a lot more energy to get everything done. Expectations themselves have a way of slowing people down and making them feel exhausted. If you never take the time to address this, you are going to find yourself constantly feeling overwhelmed and overworked. Learn to take the pressure off of yourself and give yourself permission to take it easy. Book time off, stop saying yes to everything, and delegate some of your tasks so that you do not have to attempt to do so much by yourself. The more you can work on navigating things in a less stressful manner, the less pressure you are going to feel, and therefore the less anxiety you are likely going to feel, too.

Chapter 36 Manage Excessive Anger

How often do you feel furious yet don't have a clue why? How regularly do you become forceful and make statements you don't generally mean, and afterward feel agitated and remorseful a short time later? Comparative occasions happen to the majority of us, sooner or later, and we neglect to comprehend the reasons.

Regularly, the appropriate response has to do with extreme weight that has caused you stress, which has gone to outrage as you understand that you seem to have lost control of the circumstance. At that point, you take that outrage and dissatisfaction out on others around you. Now and then that might be your family, or if at work, your associates.

Low confidence, notwithstanding stress, can likewise be at the core of a furious upheaval. You may not recognize this factor, and it is just when you begin to endure the outcomes of that low self-esteem that you may start to investigate the main driver inside yourself.

Losing control is only one way that low confidence shows itself in your conduct. "Why me? It's not reasonable!" is a typical furious upheaval for those experiencing low confidence and sentiment of regularly being the unfortunate casualty in specific conditions.

At the point when we become furious, we moved toward becoming overwhelmed by seen foul play, and afterward, we lose our emphasis on the main thing. At work, we may feel as though we are picked-upon, and in our connections, we may see a shortcoming in others where none truly exists. Maybe we see life through a red dimness - a fog that is outrage.

Defusing Anger

Defusing personal resentment may require the assistance of an expert advisor. However, you can also call upon an esteemed companion who is a decent audience and who will empower you to talk through your anger. That can be done regardless of whether it involves some yelling or crying in disappointment. Drawing out what you feel away from any detectable hindrance is a fantastic technique for looking at your attitude and your disappointment.

Once in a while, getting to the underlying driver of outrage and investigating low confidence issues, requires time and tolerance. Low confidence frequently comes from youth occasions at home or school. Absence of applause and disparagement are essential wellsprings of low confidence, in adolescence. Having the option to place them into setting and managing the resentment that has developed over numerous years is basic.

Outrage can be a risky and unsatisfactory feeling, particularly in the working environment. It can prompt upheavals of anger that could end in brutality, and if your conduct truly ends up troublesome and unsuitable, you can wind up losing your employment.

These are my preferred outrage, the executive's tips:

- If you feel yourself beginning to lose control and you need to yell at somebody, attempt to leave the circumstance. On the off chance that you, at that point, do some profound breathing activities for at any rate five minutes, in a calm spot, you will feel your displeasure begin to scatter. You should then attempt to excuse why you were so angry and afterward come back to what you were doing in advance.

- We all will think we are in every case right, in any event, when we are off-base! The arrangement is to allow others to express their assessments: to effectively tune in to what is being said and afterward to utilize levelheaded discourse to analyze the contention as opposed to losing control and yelling. I realize this is regularly simpler said than done. It takes practice; however, it works.

- In gatherings, be aware that raised voices can rapidly prompt clash. Monitor your sentiments - know about your non-verbal communication - outrage is effectively transmitted through activities and outward appearance, just as proper words.

- Before any passionate upheaval, tally to ten, and when you arrive, you may have diffused the displeasure within yourself.

Nonetheless, if there is an example of angry upheavals, for example, every day, at that point, this likely could be an ideal opportunity to look for proficient restorative counsel as your body may have an unevenness that expects tests to learn the reason. In any case, don't disregard it.

To deal with your annoyance successfully, there will be many things you'll have to think about first. Above all, it is crucial to understand that blowing up is really ordinary and in some cases, even sound. It is the point at which you begin to go overboard to circumstances and lash out at individuals in destructive manners, both to yourself as well as other people, that it turns into an issue. This article will give you some various approaches to take care of this issue and in the long run, become a specialist at controlling your feelings in some random circumstance you are in.

The initial step you will need to take is to distinguish those circumstances and individuals that make it hard to control your anger. At the point when you do this, you will be focusing on those occasions that make you the most troubled, so you can think of successful techniques for dealing with your outrage. You must understand that you will always be unable to dispense with sentiments of anger from your life. Yet, you will have the option to, in the end, control yourself totally and decrease the recurrence of those minutes when you become disturbed and angry.

At the point when you have a rundown of various approaches to monitoring yourself, it is simpler for you to deal with different circumstances that typically aggravate you. On the off chance that one strategy doesn't work, you can attempt another. It's significant that you consider and practice whatever the number of these as could reasonably be expected, so when the crucial point in time of truth shows up, you will have the option to control yourself.

Certain breathing activities have been demonstrated to have any effect when you are losing control. Taking long and full breaths flood oxygen into the body and send it to your cerebrum, making a quieting vibe that will assist you with managing your feelings when you sense that you have no power over them. Significantly, you practice these also with the goal for them to be as viable as conceivable at helping you deal with your resentment.

It is better at that point to prevent this to outrage from emerging in any case - by adequately 'dealing with our displeasure' - by remaining quiet, so we don't get to this phase of the annoyance cycle. In this article, I will accordingly give some straightforward; however, compelling procedures for remaining quiet that can be used in many circumstances.

Strategies to Cope with Immediate Stress and Anger

Leave THE SOURCE OF ANGER: By remaining close to any wellspring of stress and outrage, frequently include more pressure and outrage without us doing anything. That can be an individual, item, or circumstance causing the resentment and can be in any condition from home, work environment, or on our day by day ventures. If at all conceivable, my best counsel is to attempt to expel ourselves from this pressure. It may mean pardoning oneself from the circumstance; for example, if the load is being brought about by a relative during supper, we could forgive ourselves and leave the room before getting excessively irate. In a working environment circumstance, it may be the case that the report we have been composing for as far back as two hours is turning out badly. Rather than battling further while tired and committing more errors - just adding to the pressure; we could have a break, either by leaving the workplace, getting an espresso - or if this is beyond imagination even basically sitting at the PC and having a speedy look at the web for a couple of moments to loosen up ourselves.

Quiet DOWN BY USING DEEP BREATHING: One of the indications of expanded pressure and outrage is a reviving of the breath brought about by expanded pulse, prompting the blood requiring more oxygen, requiring snappier breath - and in that capacity the cycle proceeds. By breathing gradually, we can break this cycle and enable ourselves to quiet down. The procedure here is to take long full breaths in through the nose, hold these for a second and afterward remove a long full breath from the mouth for a few seconds, rehashing the cycle for a while. This timespan changes relying upon how focused on we are yet additionally to what extent we need to play out this action. The facts may confirm that we have the opportunity to do this in the lift before we meet someone, so twenty seconds might be all we have. At the opposite finish of the scale, we may have 10-15 or more minutes to extra. Regardless of to what extent, doing this in any event, for a couple of moments, can help offer some relief from the resentment and for longer than a couple of moments can significantly diminish individual feelings of anxiety.

Envision A RELAXING EXPERIENCE WE HAVE HAD OR SOMETHING CALMING: When feeling pushed, envision a circumstance in the past where we have felt loose, can help loosen up our brain. Additionally, pondering nothing at all can likewise be similarly as compelling, if not more so. When doing this, attempt to not consider anything by any stretch of the imagination - something that sounds simple yet marginally progressively hard to do practically speaking. Effectively utilizing both these systems takes practice, yet once accomplished, the outcomes can be powerful. For sure, in the same way as other 'quieting' procedures, these are best when used in calm spots: it can be at our work area when the workplace is vacant, or sitting on the transport to and from work, or having a stroll along the road when alone. It abandons saying that this strategy ought not to be used when we require full focus or when we are in a domain where we should be alert.

Long haul Techniques

The following arrangement of methods for quieting us is 'long haul.' By this, I mean progressing things that we can do to constrain pressure and outrage - to prevent these from working up in any case by accomplishing certain items over a more drawn out timeframe.

Ensure THAT WE GET REGULAR EXERCISE AND A HEALTHY BALANCED DIET: Regular exercise isn't fundamental for our physical wellbeing and prosperity yet additionally for our emotional wellness. Practice enables our mind to create more dopamine (a natural stimulant), which thus helps our state of mind and makes us feel more joyful. Taking customary exercise at that point helps our general state of mind incredibly. Taking approximately 30 minutes of activity - including strolling at a quick pace-every day can enormously confine our pressure and outrage levels while making us more advantageous physically. Consolidate this with a sound adjusted eating routine, and the outcomes can be much increasingly excellent. While it is past the transmit of this article to go into diet and which nourishments ought to be eaten and in what amounts, guidance for this exists in numerous different spots. Doing this can have a checked effect upon by, and substantial feelings of anxiety and can keep us physically more beneficial all the while.

Attempt TO GET A GOOD NIGHT SLEEP: This most likely sounds clear, yet I will state it at any rate. A decent night rest (ideally 7-9 hours for grown-ups) and around 9-10 hours for kids are prescribed for general wellbeing. It helps me to remember a familiar saying I once found out about resting times, 'commonly 5, by custom 7, by apathy 9 and insidiousness 11'. We are, for the most part, people and have our very own favored length of rest. While it is difficult in our bustling lives to get 8 hours of the night - and considerably increasingly hard for kids, particularly in their high school years-for us all, it is fundamental that we get these prescribed long stretches of rest every night. Similarly significant is that we get into an ordinary resting design. By getting our full amount of rest, we will be increasingly conscious during the day, less drained and in that capacity have improved fixation, all prompting less pressure and outrage.

Attempt TO HAVE PERSONAL RELATION TIME EVERY DAY: Again, this is something hard to accomplish in our bustling day by day plans, yet taking even 20-30 minutes out of every day to accomplish something that we appreciate can assist (a) with relaxing our psyche and (b) with going about as a stimulant enabling us to feel more joyful. We may think that we are too occupied to even think about taking this break, feeling that we are progressively beneficial accomplishing different things. While this might be valid, by not having this unwinding 'switch-off' time over a time of days, we just become increasingly worn out and less gainful - prompting things not be done appropriately, not getting round to tasks and accordingly getting to be pushed. That thus can promptly provoke displeasure.

BE Organized AND TRY NOT TO LET THINGS BUILD-UP: This is the last suggestion I am going to give here. Being sorted out is the bedrock of casual life. Disorder - regardless of whether this is through leaving bills unpaid, beginning for work past the point of no return, or being late for arrangements all lead to abrupt undesirable pressure and outrage - harming our wellbeing yet having a dramatic and contrary effect on our own and business relations. My best exhortation is to attempt to keep awake to date with everything from administrative work: accounts: arrangements and leave an abundant measure of time for doing these exercises. Sometimes, in order to maintain a distance from stress, we have to go out 20 minutes sooner or commit a particular day at regular intervals to sort out our accounts. Whatever this might be, we must remain composed to battle life stresses and the subsequent displeasure these can bring.

Like there is a day and night the same way, we have different sides to our feelings. There are glad feelings, and there are dim feelings. Dim feelings are a piece of what your identity is, and they give input about what is occurring you throughout everyday life.

We experience different feelings at various times of life. Every emotion works unexpectedly. For instance, dread and outrage invigorate you to activity, though misery and blame go about as depressants. In case we don't express or address these feelings, they will develop to the point of wild ejection. On the off chance that you harbor outrage inside you, you will undoubtedly explode the spread one day and lose everything all the while. That is our dim feeling; however, that doesn't mean it shouldn't have been managed.

When you are furious with somebody, you have to express your resentment adequately. It's not generally the most straightforward activity; however, it's the correct method to channel your annoyance and accomplish positive outcomes out of an adverse circumstance.

First, you ought to comprehend the contrast between grumble and analysis. In case you have an issue with your partner, or any other person, it's critical to know how you are going to deal with it. The analysis leaves the other individual inclination genuinely charged and guarded, which incites them to assault you back. The endless loop or assaults will begin, and you won't have the option to pass on the point you at first began to, and it might make you much angrier and progressively disappointed.

There are unquestionably issues in the majority of our lives that are difficult to manage, and we may require some outside help in achieving them. Outrage is one that undoubtedly hangs out in my brain. It's a terrible passionate response to something that makes us feel awful, agitated, baffled, and an entire slew of different things that we more often than do whatever it takes not to stay away from in regular daily existence. The significant thing here is to recall that you aren't the only one, and we will cover approaches to deal with your resentment, so it doesn't oversee you.

Outrage is communicated through a wide range of means extremely subject to the individual or individual doing the communication. A few of us are unquestionably more significant at managing outrage than others. A few of us are ready to get it off our chests by conversing with a companion or relative, while others brush it off and attempt to remain concentrated on other significant exercises.

The significant thing secured above is managing outrage with regards to other individuals. How precisely we are communicating it to other individuals is the worry. If it is through general discussion, that is a specific something, however, when we start to take it out on others is the point at which the connection is crossed, and an adverse action is then occurring.

You can certainly do something specific to help with controlling your outrage and the methods in which you express it. If you imagine that you have an annoying issue that you can only with significant effort oversee, then it is unquestionably prescribed to look for advising. Advising ought to never be taken as an awful choice if you imagine that it is in certainty good.

Chapter 37 Cognitive Behavioral Treatments for Anxiety and Depression

Treating Anxiety Disorders with Therapy

It doesn't matter whether you are suffering from an incapacitating phobia, panic attacks, unrelenting worries or obsessive thoughts, what is more, important is that you don't have to live a life full of anxiety and fear. Anxiety and fear be treated. Therapy is the most effective option for your anxiety problem. The reason why anxiety therapy is the best option is that it differs from other anxiety medication in many ways. Anxiety therapy focuses on treating anxiety beyond just symptoms of the problem because it uncovers the main underlying causes of your fears and worries; and then teaches you how to overcome these worries and fears. Anxiety therapy will teach you how to relax, how to look at a situation from a different perspective and in less frightening ways and in the end, you will be able to develop skills on how to cope and solve your problems. In other words, therapy will give you the best tools for overcoming anxiety as well as teach you how to use these tools.

Anxiety therapy should always be tailored towards the specific symptoms and diagnosis a particular patient presents. Usually, the length depends on the severity level of a patient's social anxiety disorder. Many anxiety therapies, as observed by the American Psychological Association, are usually relatively short-term, and most people tend to indicate significant improvements within eight therapeutic sessions. Their several therapies approach for treating social anxiety and the leading approaches to treating social anxiety are Metacognitive Therapy (MCT) and Cognitive Behavioural Therapy (CBT). We can use each of these anxiety therapy treatments separately or by combining them with other therapeutic approaches. Basically, anxiety therapy can be done either to an individual or to a group of individuals having the same anxiety problems. Irrespective of the anxiety therapy chosen, the goal still remains the same; lowering your anxiety level, overcome your fears, and calm your mind.

CBT (Cognitive Behavioral Therapy)

This therapy is best-preferred approach and widely adopted for the treatment of anxiety disorders. Most researches have shown that CBT is a very effective therapeutic approach for treating social anxiety disorder and panic disorder. Basically, Cognitive behavioral therapy focused on addressing the negative thought patterns and thought distortions that affect the way we perceive ourselves and the world around us. Just as suggested by its name, CBT consists of two main components

Cognitive therapy: Cognitive therapy focuses on examining how our negative thoughts make us anxious.

Behavior therapy: Behavior therapy focuses on how an individual responds to or behaves when faced with anxiety triggering situations.

CBT bases itself on the fact that the way we feel is determined by how we think and not by external events. This means that the situation you are in does not determine your feelings. How you feel (your feelings) are determined by how you perceive the situation you are in. Here is a case where you have been invited to a big party. In mind, you are thinking about this invitation in different ways. As you think, there are emotions you will have.

First thought: This party is going to have a lot of fun. I just love it because there will be many people and I will make new friends.

Your emotions: You will feel eager, excited and happy

Second thought: I generally don't like parties. I prefer to have to stay indoors and watch some movies or code.

Your Emotions: Neutral

Third Thought: I have never been to a party; what will I do when told to speak or when told to dance. I also don't know how to dress. People will laugh at me.

Your Emotions: You will feel sad or anxious.

Clearly, these three thoughts can make an individual have three different emotions. Our emotions depend on what we believe in, attitudes, and individual expectations. More often, individuals with anxiety disorders have a negative manner of thinking, and actually, this is what propagates negative emotions which in turn yields to fear and anxiety. Cognitive-behavioral therapy for anxiety has the main goal of identifying and correcting the negative beliefs and thoughts that a person with an anxiety disorder has.

Cognitive-behavioral therapy bases its treatment on ensuring that you change your ways of thought as one way of changing how you feel.

- CBT will teach you how to recognize when you are anxious and how that makes your body feel

- CBT will teach you coping skills as well as techniques to use so as to feel relaxed as one way of countering panic and anxiety.

- CBT will teach you how to confront your fears both in real life and in your imaginations.

Metacognitive Therapy (MCT)

In almost our daily activities, there are times that we are overwhelmed by negative thoughts, and we tend to believe in these negative thinking. However, it is not everyone who develops sustained anxiety, emotional suffering, or depression. Therefore, I would like to begin by asking yourself, what it that controls your thoughts is and what is it that determines whether you can dismiss these thoughts or what is it that makes these thoughts sink in and make you have even a prolonged and deeper distress.

We will try to offer an answer to these questions by looking at metacognition. Both healthy and unhealthy controls of the mind are based on metacognition. Metacognition bases on principle that; an individual's emotions and the control over these emotions are not determined by what a person thinks about is determined by how a person thinks. Let's look at thinking like some large orchestra activity which has many players and many instruments. In such a case, an acceptable overture can only be produced when there are a conductor and a music score. Therefore, in the human mind, metacognition is the conductor and the score behind thinking. In other words, we can say that metacognition is like cognition to cognition. Metacognition is responsible for controlling, monitoring, and appraising your awareness.

Emotional discomfort is transitory in most people because they have learned flexible ways with which they can deal with negative thoughts and beliefs constructed by their minds. The metacognitive approach bases on the idea that we become trapped in our emotional disturbance due to the fact that our metacognitions causes e a particular pattern with which we respond to our inner experiences responsible for maintaining our emotions and strengthening of the negative ideas we have. The pattern that should, therefore, be looked into is the cognitive attentional syndrome (CAS). This pattern consists of fixated attention, worry, unhelpful coping behaviors, unhelpful strategies for self-regulation, and ruminations.

Metacognitive therapy bases on the principle that metacognition plays a critical role in the understanding of the operation of cognition and how cognition generates the conscious experiences that people have for themselves and the world around them. Metacognition is responsible for shaping what we pay attention to as well as the factors that enter our consciousness. Metacognition is also responsible for shaping our appraisals and influencing the different strategies we have to adopt while regulating our thoughts and feelings.

The nature of metacognitive therapy

Metacognition basically describes a range of interrelating factors which consists of cognitive process or any knowledge involved in the control of monitoring, interpretation, and control of cognition. Metacognitive therapy is therefore divided into three; exploring knowledge and beliefs, exploring experiences and then coming up with effective strategies.

i. Knowledge and Beliefs

Metacognitive therapy begins by examining the beliefs and theories that people tend to have in their thoughts. We are in a society where some thoughts or actions are linked to some beliefs. For example, there are cases where you may feel that your religion does not allow you to have some thoughts as that would lead you to punishment because they are such thoughts are sinful. These are some of the beliefs that will affect your thoughts if you hold on to them. Metacognitive therapy will exploit two types of metacognitive knowledge; first, we will exploit your explicit or declarative beliefs and secondly we will exploit your implicit or procedural beliefs. Implicit and procedural knowledge basically represents an individual's thinking skills.

a. Explicit knowledge

This is what you can express verbally. For example, you can say. "If I continue to be with this worry, I will get depressed and may have even had a heart attack.";" I don't like the way they looked at me and laugh. I think they are seeing me as incapable." Therefore, a patient will be asked to try to express all his worries verbally to be noted.

b. Implicit knowledge

This type of knowledge cannot be expressed verbally. They can be seen as the programs or rules guiding how we think. For instance, implicit knowledge guides things like allocation of attention, use of heuristics when coming up with judgments and memory search.

c. Positive metacognitive beliefs

These are beliefs that are associated with thoughts that benefit an individual. In this case, an individual need to examine all his positive thoughts and focus his/her attention on them. For example, one can say that "Worrying about the coming exam will make me read, and when I read, I will pass my exams."

d. Negative metacognitive beliefs

These are beliefs that are associated with uncontrollability, and such beliefs will make an individual have dangerous thoughts relating to feeling worthless. For example, one can have dangerous thoughts like " I am wondering how of late I can't remember names, I think I have a brain tumor."

ii. Experiences

Metacognitive experiences focus on exploring situations that changed an individual's feelings on his/her mental status. Experiences are based on an individual's subjective feelings. In Metacognitive therapy attempts to control an individual's thinking, particularly the thoughts that raise the negative appraisals of feelings. Strategies

iii. Metacognitive strategies

Metacognitive strategies provide the best responses for controlling and altering an individual's thinking in relation to the regulation of emotions and cognition. These strategies focus on suppressing or changing the nature of an individual's cognitive activities. Negative emotions and thoughts can be reduced by altering some aspects of cognition. In this way, an individual can be made to have positive thoughts as one way of distracting or suppressing the distressing thoughts and emotions.

Adopting the Metacognitive Model of GAD

For normal people, negative thoughts are things that come and go and will not raise any negative response that will, in turn, affect them. However, there are people who when they have negative thoughts, they end up having worrying. General anxiety disorder model tries to help such individuals avoid such thoughts, anticipate the problems related to such thoughts, or find a solution to such thoughts. We look at about an individual's worry on physical self, social, and world. The metacognitive model of GAD tries to link worrying to positive metacognitive beliefs. In most cases, despite people worrying occasionally, many people have positive beliefs in relation to worrying. The metacognitive model, however, makes an assumption that self-regulation and emotional problems can be caused by over-reliance on worry as a way of trying to respond to negative thinking. Therefore, worrying can significantly contribute to a non-specific vulnerability on your emotions. General anxiety disorder develops the moment you start; you start activating and developing negative beliefs. More often, these beliefs are formed when we are exposed to interpretations of internal events or exposed to some information.

How Will Anxiety Therapy Work for You?

Anxiety has no fast solution. You can only be able to overcome an anxiety disorder when you take your time and be committed towards it. You are required to be ready to face your fears rather than avoiding them.

Therefore, be ready to feel worse so as to get better. It is important that you stick with the treatment plan and follow the advice of your therapist. There are times that you will almost feel discouraged with your recovery pace maybe because it is taking time. I think one thing you should know is that anxiety therapy is very effective when conducted at a slower pace. Be patient, and you will see the benefits. As an individual, you can focus on supporting your own anxiety therapy by being smart and taking positive steps and choices. Anxiety is affected by everything in you and around you, ranging from your daily activities to social lifestyle. Be a person who is able to make conscious decisions that will make you more relaxed; develop a more positive mental outlook and vitality in your daily life.

It is appropriate that you learn more about anxiety. You cannot overcome a problem without knowing the problem. Advance your knowledge of anxiety. This is where MCT and CBT education is applied. However, education alone is not enough to cure anxiety disorder but rather will play a very important role in ensuring that you fully benefit from the therapy.

Try to promote your connections with other people. Isolation and loneliness create an effective platform for anxiety. Just ensure that you reach to others and socialize more so as to decrease your vulnerability to anxiety. Make new friends, visit them frequently, and choose your loved ones whom you can freely share your concerns and worries with. You can also join support groups or self-help groups.

It is also appropriate that you adopt healthy lifestyle habits. It is advisable that you include physical activity or exercise in your daily activities because this is one way of relieving anxiety tension. Never use stimulants, drugs, and alcohol to enable you to cope with anxiety symptoms as this may even turn worse.

Reduce stress or don't associate with things stressing you. Take your time and examine your life. Identify those thoughts or events that make you feel stressed. Find a solution to those you can and avoid the rest that you cannot. If there are people who make you feel anxious, be ready to avoid them. Also, be bold to say no to extra responsibilities added to you. Always ensure that you make time to relax and have fun.

Mindfulness is the practice of being fully aware of where you are and what you are doing, and not being overwhelmed by the things around you. Every person has the innate capability of being mindful, but it becomes strong when you practice it on a daily basis.

Whenever you develop awareness for what you're doing either through your senses or thoughts and emotions, you are being mindful. Research shows that mindfulness modifies brain structure and improves the quality of our lives.

For a person suffering from depression or anxiety, they have a much better chance of reducing the symptoms by indulging in mindfulness. The following are some tips for practicing mindfulness:

- Set aside some time: start by setting aside some time for practicing mindfulness meditation. The beauty of mindfulness is that you don't have to incur an expense. But you have to allocate some time-resource. This is ideally the time you are most comfortable and are at peace with yourself. You have to honor this schedule no matter what you may be doing.

- Improve your observation skills: mindfulness is about being aware of what's happening around you. Thus, you have to be pretty aware of your surroundings. Ensure that you develop your observation skills so that you can be able to tell what's going on around you. With great observation skills, nothing will escape your notice.

- Let go your judgments: it is in human nature to judge different things that we see. But in this state of mindfulness, you must not let yourself be influenced by your judgments. Just take the role of the observer and watch your judgments go by.

- Fight distractions: there are many instances in which we are distracted by a variety of things. Once distractions come into the scene, they carry your focus away. Thus, you must ensure that you have laser focus, and keep your mind to the present moment.

- Notice your contributions: learn to recognize the role you play in your environment. By identifying the things that are as a result of your doings, it strengthens your power of introspection.

Mindfulness exercises for anxiety and depression

The following mindfulness exercises are aimed at helping a person overcome their anxiety:

1. Mindfulness breathing

This exercise is perhaps the commonest exercise in mindfulness. It is very effective in eliminating distress, and fighting both anxiety and depression. The beauty of this exercise is that virtually anyone can practice it, and all you have to do is find somewhere peaceful for your daily ritual. You can also perform the exercise quickly whenever you are overwhelmed. It starts by assuming a comfortable position. Some people might stand, sit by a window, or even lie on a bed. You are the one that knows what position is most comfortable. Once you get into that position, close your eyes, and put both hands on your chest. And then you may begin to breathe in and out slowly. As you expel your breath, ensure that you focus on your thoughts, and resist the urge to fight the bad thoughts. This act alone is enough to get rid of the bad emotions and fears.

2.   The raisin exercises

This exercise is performed at the introductory stages. It basically tests various senses of an individual. Anyone can perform this exercise. It starts with putting a raisin in front of you and observing a variety of things:

- How it looks
- How it feels
- How it smells
- How it tastes

By focusing on the raisin, you are in a position to bring your mind to the present moment.

3.   The body scans

This is another exercise that doesn't require much in order to perform. First off, the participant must lie on their back, with their palms facing up, and their feet held slightly apart. In that state, the participant may be still, listening to the sensations of their body, and paying attention to how their skin feels against different things. They may take a deep breath and expel the breath in slight gasps, exploring the contents of their mind. The participant uses either palm alternately to scan various parts of their body while they "listen" to the sensations that are elicited.

4.   Mindful seeing

Vision plays a big role in the art of mindfulness. Thus, it necessitates this exercise. Mindful seeing heightens a person's awareness and helps them understand their present reality. It starts with sitting by a window and looking out, where there's the light of a city. Start looking at the different things that are emitting lights in the city and fight the urge to label them. By allowing yourself to notice all these lights, you will relieve yourself of emotional burdens and getting started to conquer your anxiety and depression.

5.   Mindfulness watching your thoughts

The average person has many thoughts coasting through their mind at any given time. Some thoughts can pass by and they won't be aware. But when you engage in mindfulness watching of your thoughts, you are in a position to understand how your brain works. Start off by assuming a comfortable position, preferably a lying position, facing up the ceiling. You can put on some soothing instrumental music for effect. Then close your eyes and start watching your thoughts. Fight the urge to label those thoughts and take the role of the observer. This exercise will not only relieve you of anxiety and depression but it will help you understand how you perceive various things.

6.   Mindfulness preparation for sleep

The problem with having anxiety or depression is that it takes away a person's ability to fall asleep quickly. The affected person might jump into bed but they will stay awake for a very long time. But thanks to mindfulness, you actually have a chance to sleep as fast as you would hope. It starts with you taking a shower and putting on your sleeping clothes and then climbing atop your bed with your eyes facing up. Focus on the ceiling above and envision your mind as an empty vessel. Slowly, start filling up your mind with light, and watch as the vessel slowly gets filled up with whiteness. It will create a hypnotized sensation that will promptly put you to sleep.

Chapter 39 Powerful Steps to Self-Love

Most of us have grown up thinking that we need others to love who we are so that we can be happy. Wanting others to love you is no bad goal. However, if you're going to stop at nothing in order to be loved, if you're going to let others have their way at your expense, then that's unfair to yourself—and ultimately, you're going to be mad at both yourself and the world. Self-love is treating yourself as you would a good friend. It is about satisfying your needs and forgiving yourself. Self-love is associated with the following:

Low Anxiety

Depression

More Happiness

More Optimism

Healthy Habits

Happiness

The following are some of the practices that boost self-love:

Start Your Day on a Positive Note

Start your day by telling yourself something that will put a smile on your face. When you hit your day off on a positive note, you get to take on other activities of the day with a positive mindset. You can start the day by reminding yourself of how well you handled a situation, the important role that you play in someone's life or in a company, and so on.

Eat Healthy Foods

Research has shown that there's a correlation between the foods we eat and our emotional state. If we eat unhealthy foods, such as junk foods, we are more likely to be stressed out and anxious as compared to if we eat a meal consisting of nutritious ingredients. Food is our fuel. For the optimal functioning of our body, we need to consume food that will nourish us, and provide us with the energy to complete various tasks. Healthy meals encourage us to cook our meals at home, instead of eating out, thus saving money.

Workout

The more fit you are, the more likely you are to experience happy feelings and have high self-esteem. But if your body is in terrible shape, you are likely to suffer low self-esteem, and it will contribute to making poor decisions. Get into the habit of working out regularly. The following are some of the benefits associated with exercising:

Improved Heart Health

Improved Blood Circulation

Improved Brain Health

Improved Sleep Quality

Improved Moods

There are various ways, both expensive and inexpensive, to get started on working out.

Silence Your Inner Critic

There's an inner critic inside each one of us that complicates things. This critic is harsh on us and makes us feel terrible. We should make a point of silencing this critic before they do us major harm. But this doesn't mean we should ignore any form of criticism.

Surround Yourself with Positive People

They say that a person is the average of the five people they spend the most time with. True. Make a point of spending time with only positive individuals. This will make you take on their positive traits and help you become better at making decisions.

Stop Comparing Yourself with Others

There will always be people more successful and less successful than you. But more importantly, success can adhere to your own definition. Have your own idea of success. Comparing yourself to other people will take away your self-worth when you come up short.

Cut Off Toxic People

Toxic people are nothing more than energy vampires. They will steal away your positive energy and leave you feeling terrible. Make a point of getting rid of them. Of course, it is not easy to distance yourself from toxic people – especially if you have been the energy supply – but take baby steps first, like refusing to hang out with them, and then large steps like changing residence.

Celebrate Your Wins

There's nothing like "a small win." If you make a step forward, always get into a celebratory mood. Being grateful to yourself will allow you to tap into the whole of your potential. Winning in small ways will instill a winning mindset into your subconscious, and you are far more likely to achieve most of your goals.

Step Out of Your Comfort Zone

As long as you're in your comfort zone, you will never know what you're really capable of. Push yourself out of your comfort zone and watch your life turn around. Success is always found in the extra effort that we apply. If you are looking for a life partner, try to meet more people, instead of locking yourself away and complaining that there are no suitable partners.

Embrace Your Quirkiness

If you have some traits that are considered "out of the norm," you should embrace them, instead of being ashamed of them. If you stand tall with your quirkiness, you will draw people in. There will be a sense of uniqueness about you.

Follow Your Passion

It's the one thing that excites you, but at the same time, you're scared of failing. Overcome your fear of failure and go for your passion. Many successful people have revealed that their secret to success is merely following what they are most passionate about.

Help Others

By helping others, we get a huge sense of fulfillment. It is incredibly satisfying to lighten the burden of other people. It is also a form of networking. Life is interconnected. At one point, you may require something and find yourself needing the expertise of the person that you helped, in which case it will be rendered easily.

Strengthen Your Relationships

You're not resourceful enough to stay on your own. You will always depend on others, particularly your life partner. Work on strengthening your close relationships so that you can enjoy abundant peace of mind and support.

Give Up the Need for the Approval of Others

No matter what you do, there will always be someone to find fault with it. Desist from trying to be in everyone's good book. Think about it; when everyone likes you, you won't have anyone to prove yourself to, and your success will be kind of bland. Do you know why Sylvester Stallone feels so great about himself? It's because he received a lot of rejection before he finally got his breakthrough. And now he feels great knowing that all those executives that shunned him have helplessly seen him become a star.

Now you have reached the end of this book, but not the end of your CBT journey. These pages have prepared you to use CBT to transform your mind and consequently your life. That does not mean that your journey is over; rather, it has just begun. CBT is your best friend. It is a companion that you should carry with you through the rest of your life. Keep using it to see marked changes in how you approach life and how you feel.

Here is a wrap up of everything covered in this book:

Avoiding situations that bring you harm is great. But in real life, we both know that that is not always realistic. Life throws plenty of bad situations at you and you can't avoid them all. Therefore, it is essential to develop healthy coping skills for when you do encounter these situations.

Situations that stir up mental illness symptoms can be everyday situations that other, healthier people find to be no big deal. But for you, they can feel catastrophic. They can lead you to relapse in your symptoms, after working so hard to overcome those symptoms with

CBT. Learning to cope in harmful everyday situations is essential to keep yourself from falling into despair.

Anxiety

Many everyday situations that are nothing to healthy people can trigger severe anxiety in some. For instance, a huge crowd at an airport can be stressful for anyone, but it can be disastrous for you if you have agoraphobia or social anxiety. But what if you have to fly for work or to visit a sick relative? You have to be a part of that airport crowd, whether you like it or not. The situation is not ideal for you but you can use various techniques to cope with your anxiety.

The best technique is relaxation. Focus on your breathing. Breathe in through your nose, out through your mouth. By focusing on your breathing, you take your mind off of the stress that surrounds it.

Progressive muscle relaxation also is helpful in anxiety-provoking situations. Start first from the muscles in your scalp. Force yourself to relax those muscles. Next move to your forehead muscles. Keep roving your mind over your body, forcing the relaxation of each of your muscle groups. The relaxation will calm you and the intense mental focus required to perform this exercise will take your mind off of your stress.

Some people find tapping to be soothing. You can repeat a mantra to yourself such as, "I will survive this. This is really not so bad" as you tap different parts of your body. The physical action of tapping paired with the repeated affirmation can help trick your mind into believing what you are saying to yourself.

Sometimes anxiety can impair your ability to focus on anything. In that case, it is essential to pick a spot on the wall and focus on it intently. Do not chase any other thoughts that enter your head. That spot on the wall is your refuge. Use it to take your mind off of the craziness raging around you and within you.

Facing Your Fears

CBT is great for helping you overcome irrational fears and phobias. This is because CBT allows you to think about your phobias and understand that they are not rational and not conducive to your peace of mind.

If you have a phobia, you may find it very helpful to write about your phobia. When it is on paper, you will begin to see how silly it really is. If you are scared of airplanes, what are the odds of a crash, really? You are far more likely to die in a car crash than a plane crash.

If you are scared of dogs because of a traumatic encounter with a dog in your childhood, remember that most dogs are man's best friends and that you are a lot bigger now. Analyze your fears to see how scary they really are.

To truly overcome your phobia, you need to begin to condition yourself to it. Exposing yourself to what scares you can help teach your mind to stop fearing it as it witnesses you emerge unscathed. There are classes you can take to condition yourself to overcome fear of heights, flying, and other phobias. Consider going to the snake or spider exhibit at a local zoo to stand near the creatures that make you want to scream. You will begin to realize that your phobias do not hurt you. If you have social phobia, try taking brief walks outside and striking up a brief conversation with one stranger a day.

The above relaxation techniques can also really help you when you are feeling the vise grip of fear from a phobia. Breathe, focus, and use progressive muscle relaxation to bring yourself out of your fear.

Handling Depression

The hardest part of coping with depression is that depression cripples your will to do anything. You may not even have the energy to get out of bed, let alone perform CBT on yourself. But coping with your depression gets easier when you begin to change your thinking to more positive thoughts. Positive thinking has the ability to release feel-good hormones like serotonin in your brain, allowing you to feel better and begin to move forward with your life.

When you find yourself drowning in depression symptoms, there may be a reason that you feel so blue. Maybe life is just hard right now or you have not been taking care of your body. Try to identify the source of your depression and remove it from your life. Focus on the present and enjoying life right now. Life is too short to be spent suffering in your bed.

Anger Management

If you have trouble managing your anger, you need to step back and breathe when you start to see red. Use your CBT journal to write down why a situation made you mad enough to hit someone or have an outburst. Then, analyze the situation. Was it really what you thought, or were you doing something like assuming and negative labeling? Were you ignoring the positives of the situation, or of a person that angered you? Now, in the future, how can you handle this situation without hitting and throwing things and lashing out verbally? Is there something you can do that is more conducive to a reasonable solution?

Rarely is anger ever a solution. Uncontrolled anger can get you into a lot of trouble with loved ones and even the law. Breathe, and think of better ways to react to situations than angry outbursts.

Using CBT to Overcome addiction

Addiction is often referred to as an illness. Many people fail to understand that addiction is usually a symptom of a deeper illness. People use drugs, alcohol, and other addictive behaviors such as gambling to create instant gratification and numb themselves against life. These addictive behaviors offer addicts temporary pleasure that drowns out the deeper pain addicts are experiencing inside of themselves. Basically, addicts use their addictions to distract themselves, or numb themselves, from what is really wrong. When the pleasure wears off, addicts literally feel like they are in hell because they have no shield from their pain, and they desperately chase a new high or thrill to keep them in the numb, pleased state that lets them ignore their problems. Addicts often live in denial of their real problems, and engage in harmful behaviors to avoid feeling the emotional fallout from their life situations, past traumas, or their childhoods.

Since CBT can address inner thoughts and thus change outer behaviors, it offers a rich opportunity for addicts to overcome their addictions. Addicts can use CBT to identify the thoughts and emotions that drive them to use and replace those thoughts and emotions with healthier ones that do not drive them to seek numbness. It also helps them learn to avoid situations, also known as triggers, which lead to relapses. In addition, addicts can use CBT to find healthy alternatives to self-medicating using substances, shopping, gambling, eating, sex, or whatever vice they have chosen to escape their problems with.

Identify addictive behaviors and the thoughts behind them. If you suddenly crave a drug, what triggered you to want to use? Was it a tense situation, like an argument with your family or a rough day at work? Did

you see someone or hear a song from your drug days
that made your brain start thinking about drugs?

Conclusion

Now, think of better ways to cope with the current situation. Maybe you can do yoga or exercise to relieve stress. Maybe just writing in your journal and taking a hot shower is all you need. Engage in healthy feel-good coping mechanisms, rather than participating in substance use. While substance use can relieve your bad feelings in the short term, it only worsens your mental health and your life circumstances in the long term.

Above all, remember your resolve to be clean and sober. You have made tremendous progress. Your life and your health are probably significantly better without drugs and alcohol playing a role in your behavior. You don't want to backtrack now and discount everything that you have accomplished. One way to deal with cravings and addiction is to remember why you wanted to get clean in the first place.

Remind yourself of the awful things about drug use that made you want to quit.

Then, think about all that you have accomplished in getting clean. You have done something that less than fourteen percent of drug users do.

CPSIA information can be obtained
at www.ICGtesting.com
Printed in the USA
LVHW020505061120
670809LV00002B/198